BLACK AWARENESS

BLACK AWARENESS

A THEOLOGY OF HOPE

MAJOR J. JONES

Abingdon Press
Nashville and New York

BLACK AWARENESS: A THEOLOGY OF HOPE

Copyright © 1971 by Abingdon Press

ISBN 0-687-03585-6

Library of Congress Catalog Card Number: 77-148067

Quotations from "Black Theology and Protestant Thought" by Geddes
Hanson are reprinted from *Social Progress*, September-October, 1969.
Published by the Board of Christian Education of The United Presby-
terian Church in the USA. Used by permission.
Material from *Black Theology and Black Power* by James H. Cone,
published by Seabury Press, 1969, is used by permission. Copyright ©
1969 by The Seabury Press.
Quotations from *Theology of Hope* by Jürgen Moltmann, published by
Harper & Row in 1967, are used by permission of the publisher.
Selections from *Before the Mayflower* by Lerone Bennett are used by
permission of the publisher, Johnson Publishing Co., Inc. Copyright
1961 and 1969.
Quotations from Vincent Harding, "The Religion of Black Power,"
published by Beacon Press in *The Religious Situation: 1968*, edited by
Donald R. Cutler, are used by permission.
Quotations from Anita Cornwell and John Killens in "Symposium on
Black Power," published in *Negro Digest*, November, 1966, are used
by permission. Quotations from Ronald Fair in the same article are
reprinted by permission of William Morris Agency, Inc. Copyright ©
1966 by the Johnson Publishing Company.
Material from *Religion, Revolution and the Future* by Jürgen Moltmann,
published in 1969 by Charles Scribner's Sons, is used by permission.
Quotations from Robert Goldston, *The Negro Revolution*, published
by The Macmillan Co. in 1968, are used by permission. Copyright ©
Robert Goldston 1968.
Parts of Chaps. 6 and 8 of this book contain material from the author's
article "Black Awareness: Theological Implications of the Concept,"
published in *Religion in Life*, Autumn, 1969. Copyright 1969 by Abingdon Press. Used by permission.

SET UP, PRINTED AND BOUND BY THE
PARTHENON PRESS, AT NASHVILLE,
TENNESSEE, UNITED STATES OF AMERICA

This book is dedicated to
my wife, Mattie
and
my daughter, Chandra
who gave me the time and inspiration needed
to prepare this book to the exclusion of many
hours which should have been theirs

Acknowledgments

This book would not have been possible without the constant nurture and inspiration which I derived from my many administrative and teaching colleagues at the Interdenominational Theological Center in Atlanta, Georgia. They contributed to this project by allowing me to test many of the ideas herein expressed against the background of their critical reactions. Their suggestions, derived from discussions, were most helpful in shaping much of the thought included in this book.

Some of this material appeared earlier in an article in *Religion and Life* entitled "Black Awareness: Theological Implications."

I am also deeply indebted to Dr. L. Harold DeWolf and Dr. Walter G. Muelder, former teachers and friends, for their counsel on many views herein expressed. However, in acknowledgement of their counsel, I must dissociate them from any responsibility for the quality or content of the final views expressed in the book, as neither of them have had the chance to read the manuscript.

My thanks also go to Mrs. Helen S. Johnson, my secretary, for typing the manuscript; and to the many publishers who allowed me to quote from books and periodicals.

Major J. Jones
Gammon Theological Seminary
Atlanta, Georgia

Contents

1

INTRODUCTION: THE CASE FOR A BLACK THEOLOGY OF HOPE

This book is offered as one of the many current expressions of what increasingly is becoming known as "black theology." While it is meant to relate generally to the current theologies of hope, it is written from a specific "black theological" frame of reference. It seeks to explore the revolutionary potential of the Christian ideas of the black man's future against a historical interpretation of the black experience. The primary concern of the book is for the future of the Christian faith; but in a more related and specific sense, it seeks to suggest a more viable future for the black man within the context of a pro-white society. No Christian theology of hope can overlook the fact that the Christian faith is wholly oriented to God as the power of the future which arrived in Jesus Christ under the signs of promise and hope for a more feasible future. Indeed, the categories of hope and futurity are at the very core of the Christian faith. Jurgen Moltmann rightly states that "there is therefore only one real problem in Christian theology, which its own object forces upon it and which it in turn forces on mankind and on human thought: the problem of the

Future." [1] Harvey Cox further asserts, "The only future that theology has, one might say, is to become the theology of the future." [2]

What is most needed today, especially for the black awareness movement, is a new correlation between the eschatological origins of Christian faith and the present revolutionary forces that seek to build a new and better future for the black man. Such a theology cannot be stated in the parlance of the current theology of hope used to express the thoughts of such men as Jurgen Moltmann, Wolfhart Pannenberg, Ernst Bloch, and others. Too much of their thought is abstract and not related to what is inherent in the thought-content of the black man's aspirations for the future. Indeed, a black theology that starts with eschatology must correlate the contents of eschatological hope with the conditions of the black experience and an intelligible understanding of the same. This task of theologizing requires an anthropology of hope, one that is oriented to the future of the black man. As Geddes Hanson of Princeton rightly puts it:

Black Theology . . . is a self-conscious effort to relate the experience of American Blackness to the corpus of Christian theology. Proceeding from the conviction that theology itself is the attempt to deal with the realities of human experience from the perspective of the divine-human negotiation, Black Theology lifts up the reality of the experience of blackness in America as being relevant to the theological task. [3]

[1] Jurgen Moltmann, *Theology of Hope* (translated by James W. Leitch, New York: Harper, 1967), p. 16.

[2] Harvey Cox, "The Death of God and the Future of Theology," *New Theology No. 4* edited by Martin E. Marty and Dean G. Peerman (New York: Macmillan, 1967), p. 252.

[3] "Black Theology and Protestant Thought," *Social Progress: A Journal of Church and Society*, September-October, 1969, p. 5.

Many white theologians have now begun to ask, "Why a Black Theology?" while remaining totally unaware of what the growing body of a wide range of black literature in general, and black theology in particular, is attempting to say. They do not accept the fact that the task of the theologizing process must also be related to the black man's quest for a more palatable future. Too many have not accepted the quest or the need for a black theology.

The traditional content of systematic theology may well not correspond to that of much of the literature of black theology. Black theology differs from traditional theology by the simple reason that it may not be as concerned to describe such traditional themes as the eternal nature of God's existence as it is to explore the impermanent, paradoxical, and problematic nature of human existence. Much of the task of black theology is to reclaim a people from humiliation, and in the process of so doing, it may well neglect such unrelated subjects as humility before man and guilt before God. If black theology is to speak realistically and cogently to a people whose lives have been worn down, whose best hopes have so often been frustrated, and who have been reminded at every turn by human word and action that they are less than worthy of so much that other ordinary humans possess, it must have a new and fresh message of hope for the future. As Geddes Hanson would further suggest, indeed does not

the truth of the theme of "new being" in Christ suggest itself as more appropriate to the meaning of the gospel in the lives of black people? In the light of the inability of the traditional mainstream theology of the church to provide a rationale for a programmatic humanizing of our society, it has become obvious to many blacks that the time has come to insist on the inadequacy of any theology that presumes to relate the fact of God to the facts of human life without accepting the peculiarities of black life as data. Black Theology brings its reflections on the black experience to the theological conference table claiming itself to be the salt without which any attempt to do theological business in America today is without savor.

Implicit in the previous remarks are the assumptions that Black Theology, in doing its job well, will force Protestant thought to the point of reconsidering its eschatology, its ecclesiology, and its anthropology. It must, in fact, do more.[4]

In a true sense then, black theology, like all theology, arises out of a people's common experiences with God. At this moment in history, the black community seeks to express itself theologically from a black frame of reference in language that speaks to the current conditions of a people. The Committee on Theological Prospectives of the National Committee of Black Churchmen put it in clear language when they said:

Black Theology is not a gift of the Christian gospel dispensed to slaves; rather it is an appropriation which the slaves made of the gospel given by their white oppressors.

. . . Black Theology is a theology of black liberation. It seeks to plumb the black condition in the light of God's revelation in Jesus Christ, so that the black community can see that the gospel is commensurate with the achievement of black humanity. Black Theology is a theology of "blackness." It is the affirmation of black humanity that emancipates black people from white racism thus providing authentic freedom for both white and black people. It affirms the humanity of white people in that it says "No" to the encroachment of white oppression.[5]

---

[4] *Ibid.*, p. 10.

[5] A statement of the National Committee of Black Churchmen produced by the Committee on Theological Prospectives issued June 13, 1969, at the Interdenominational Theological Center in Atlanta, Georgia.

Black theology has given new meaning to blackness, and it seeks to relate that blackness to a truth that is liberating; thus it becomes for many, in current times, a new light of freedom under God. Having tasted that freedom through identification with God's intention for black humanity, the black man will stop at nothing in expressing an ever stronger affirmation of black selfhood.

Black theology then may well become that truth which places a black person for the first time in touch with a deep core self which is the real; and once a man finds such a core self, he is prepared to give all for it. This is the liberating intent of black theology. If Moltmann is right in suggesting that the gospel of Christ frees a man to be for those who labor and are heavily laden, the humiliated and abused,[6] then it would seem that black theology would represent an important facet of that gospel message which Jesus brought to the world. However, black theology is but an important facet of the total appropriation of the gospel to the current issues of our time.

Dr. James H. Cone of Union Seminary states it well, in speaking of what must concern any black theology of hope, when he says:

A black theologian wants to know what the gospel has to say to a man who is jobless and cannot get work to support his family because the society is unjust. He wants to know what God's word is to the countless black boys and girls who are fatherless and motherless because white society decreed that

[6] Jürgen Moltmann, "Toward a Political Hermeneutics of the Gospel," *Union Seminary Quarterly Review*, Summer, 1968, pp. 313-14. For a larger discussion of this topic, see Chapter 5, pp. 83 ff. of Jürgen Moltmann's *Religion, Revolution and the Future* (New York: Scribner's, 1969).

blacks have no rights. Unless there is a word from Christ to the helpless, then why should they respond to him? [7]

These statements above are mere expositions of the central task of black theology, and unless it serves such a purpose, its aims have been lost and its unique responsibilities have not been met. Black theology must, above all else, be a theology of hope, it must hold within its content a promise to be redeemed within the earthly life span of those who possess such a hope and who discern such a promise. Under God, it must be a clear gospel message of new light and new self-understanding, in the ultimate, of what it means to live, even in a world of despair.

Black theology will be able to out-balance anxiety as a primary posture toward the future only in its clear exposition of a new kind of meaning to be derived from new interpretations of the black experience which can provide a sufficient reason and right for the black man to hope within the American context. We might conclude then that an adequate faith in the future can be rooted only in a secure selfhood, conceived to be authentic under God. Only such a faith opens up the horizon of the future of fulfillment—for the individual black man, for mankind as a whole, for the human history of the present, and the human history of all reality. If its gospel message is real for the black community, black theology must contend with Moltmann that "those who hope in Christ can no longer put up with reality as it is, but begin to . . . contradict it. Peace with God means conflict with the world." [8] To be adequate for the black community, black theology must bespeak a new vision; if there is no clear vision of the future, black people might easily reconcile

[7] Cone, *Black Theology and Black Power* (New York: Seabury Press, 1969), p. 43.
[8] Moltmann, A *Theology of Hope*, p. 21.

16

themselves to the present. In a real sense, without the hope that arises in the full realization of blackness, derived from an adequate theology of the black awareness movement, many black people themselves have begun to realize that conditions of black people have become intolerable. Black theology must provide them with some new words of hope; it must provide them with the will to break away from the present toward the future.[9]

More perhaps than any other, this theology of hope seeks to be a this-world interpretation; and, in this light, it seeks to look at the hope of a people from an internalized black awareness frame of reference. Though it is centered in black awareness, such a hope is under God; it is a hope seen from a black perspective.

[9] *Ibid.*, p. 100.

2

THE MEANING OF THE BLACK EXPERIENCE IN HISTORIC PERSPECTIVE

The Pre–Civil War Development of the Black Experience

Both psychologists and psychiatrists would generally agree that the black experience has created within the minds of black people a marred self-image of varying degrees which has permeated their whole beings. It is also an equally generally accepted fact that this negative self-concept has led to many self-destructive attitudes and negative behavior patterns which have often hindered the black man in his attempts to achieve equal status in America, even if such were at all possible.

To understand this negative concept problem, produced by the black experience within the context of American life, one must look at some of the historical factors that contributed to the development of such a negative self-image, self-concept, and distorted "who am I?"

Over three hundred years ago, and many years thereafter, black men, women, and children were extracted from their native land of Africa; deliberately by plan stripped bare psychologically, physically, and religiously; and transplanted in an alien land dominated by the white man. Within this new context, the black man was to occupy the most degraded of all human conditions: that of a slave—a mere piece of property, a nobody in the fullest sense of the word. The black family, by plan, was broken up, scattered, and sold from auction block to auction block all over America. The black male, for all practical purposes, was completely emasculated, and the black female was systematically exploited and vilely degraded. The plantation system implanted a subservience and dependency in the psyche of the black man that has made him traditionally much too dependent upon the goodwill and paternalism of the white man.

The cultural climate and the conscious planning, on the part of many of the white oppressors before and after slavery, have given continuity, encouragement, and stability to many of the traditional patterns of treatment of black people. Therefore, the black man is not without some justification when he contends that the white man is guilty, both by conscious participation and by indirect benefit, of much of even the current exploitation of the black man.

The black experience is all that is implied and then more. The whole period of American slavery, and what took place in America thereafter, is indeed a black experience. It has always been interesting to note that the white man attempted to gloss over all that was bad about slavery and his traditional treatment of black people by contending that the black man accepted such treatment and was happy with it. However, if any cogent words were needed to dispel such a false contention, they would be the words of Frederick Douglass, a black man who was to become a great leader in the abolition cause. Douglass was sold by his Baltimore owner in 1834 to a man named Covey, whose profession it was to "break" slaves to the point where they would be psychologically and mentally conditioned for the hard life on the slaveholders' plantations in the Deep South. Douglass' description of his life with Covey reveals the central anguish of the black experience during the period of slavery. Of his slave life, Douglass writes:

> If at any one time of my life, more than another, I was made to drink the bitterest dregs of slavery, that time was during the first six months of my stay with this man Covey. We worked all weathers. It was never too hot, or too cold; it could never rain, blow, snow, or hail too hard for us to work in the field. . . . The longest days were too short for him, and the shortest nights were too long for him. I was somewhat unmanageable at first, but a few months of this discipline tamed me. Mr. Covey succeeded in *breaking* me—in body, soul, and spirit . . . the dark night of slavery closed in upon me, and behold a man transformed to a brute!
>
> . . . I shall never be able to narrate half the mental experiences through which it was my lot to pass, during my stay at Covey's. I was completely wrecked, changed, and bewildered; goaded almost to madness at one time, and at another reconciling myself to my wretched condition.
>
> . . . I suffered bodily as well as mentally. I had neither sufficient time in which to eat, nor to sleep, except on Sunday. The overwork, and the brutal chastisement of which I was the victim, combined with that ever-gnawing and soul-devouring thought— *"I am a slave—and a slave for life—a slave with no rational ground to hope for freedom"*—rendered me a living embodiment of mental and physical wretchedness.[1]

In many ways, these words of Douglass' represent that part of the black experience which took place during the long period of slavery. One cannot glean the full meaning of the

[1] Robert Goldston, *The Negro Revolution* (New York: Macmillan, 1968), p. 67.

black experience unless he understands something of the meaning of slavery in the light of the black experience. Such a knowledge can be acquired only if slavery is seen from a black frame of reference.

The Slave Traders

Among the many people who contributed to the dehumanizing process and the subjection of the black man to the many ordeals of slavery, the persons who did most to help perpetuate the institution were the slave traders. They were the ones who provided the human cargo.

History has asked many times, Who were these men? Who were these traders in human flesh? Where did they come from?

The slave traders were hard-handed men, but generally brave. They were of all nationalities, but especially Portuguese, Spanish, Dutch, English, and American. They were respectable merchants taking on a little extra cargo, they were derelicts who had been press-ganged onto a slaver, they were adventurers eager to make a quick fortune, they were Bible-pounding preachers who had gone money mad, they were sedate clerks representing respectable commercial companies, they were pirates, and sometimes, they were mere sadists seeking satisfaction.

The risks they ran were many and deadly. There were the unchartered reefs and huge surfs of the West African Coast, which might dash their ship's hull to pieces; there were the fevers—malaria, dengue, and yellow fever—which could burn through their crews like fire through straw; there were crafty and fierce native kings, who might capture them on whim and put them to death; there were the slaves themselves, who might revolt in midpassage and massacre crews and officers; there were the pirates, who considered a slaver a rich prize;

21

and toward the end of the slave-trading days, there were the frigates and the troops of the Royal Navy beneath whose guns they might be sunk, or from whose yardarms they might be hanged. Yet the slavers came in the thousands and kept coming, more and more of them. Only the prospects of tremendous profits could have sustained their determination. And the profits were fabulous—two or three hundred percent, allowing for all the many slaves who died during the Atlantic crossing.[2]

The four centuries of the slave trade brought about the greatest forced migration in human history—a migration which, for sheer misery and human suffering as well as for profit, was without equal in human experience.[3] It is also of interest to note within this context that "the slave trade hardened and degraded almost everyone who engaged in it— from the stay-at-home merchants to the slave ship captains and the crews, to the African tribes themselves."[4]

Much more could be said of what slavery did to the white man, but too little has been said of what happened to the black man.

The Rationale for Slavery

As has been mentioned above, the slave trade and the period that followed had an adverse effect on almost everyone who engaged in it, and the white men's mentality toward the black man was most affected and impaired by its reciprocal contact with the black experience during slavery and the subsequent periods after slavery. In order to accommodate the dehumanizing process to which the black man was sub-

[2] *Ibid.*, pp. 22-23.
[3] *Ibid.*, p. 23.
[4] *Ibid.*

jected, the white mind has traditionally had to make several basic assumptions. First of all, the white mind had to conclude that the black man was not human, that he had no soul, that he was, at best, only subhuman; thus, he was not worthy of equal treatment, equal opportunity, equal place, and equal status? Second, the white mind had to find adequate theological foundations for such an assumption, so certain passages of Scripture were selected to support every facet of the dehumanizing process from the very beginning of the black-white relation in America. Genesis 9:18-29 was just one example of the many scriptures used to account for the support of the divine origin of the segregation of the races after the flood. The story relates the division of the world among the sons of Noah. Genesis 9:22-25 is used to support the fact that God cursed Ham, through Noah, and that this curse was transferred biologically to the black man; therefore, he was always to be the servant. The assumptions were that: (a) God pronounced the curse, (b) the curse was biologically transferable, (c) Ham was the original victim of the curse, (d) the children of the original victim of the curse were always to be slaves, and (e) the original victims of the curse were to be members of the Negroid race.[5] Many other passages of the Bible were used to support everything that the white man did to the black man, and yet neither the white nor the black people were fully convinced that it was right. Third, when it was conceded that the black man was human, that he did indeed possess a soul, and that he could become a Christian, it was conceded only on the added assumption that he was not equal because of his inferior men-

[5] One of the best discussions of the misuse of the Bible to support such views is Everett Tilson's book, *Segregation and the Bible* (Nashville: Abingdon Press, 1958).

tality. In addition to his inferior mental characteristics, there were the biological and physical characteristics of "blackness," which many concluded made the black man inferior to the white man. Fourth, the black man had to be kept in a subjected servant status, else his substandard economic status could not be assured. Fifth, the black family had to be kept unstable and prevented from crystallizing into a social unit, and especially deprived of a strong black male image. There had to be no climate to allow the development of a positive or confident social ego; nor was the black man, because of the white cultural context, allowed to achieve a positive personal self-confidence. The black experience, to which the black man has been subjected, is only one of the chief psychological factors that has led to the mass inertia of the black man in many areas of his life. This lack of forthright challenge to the white man, on the part of the black man, has given the white mentality a chance to become fixed and, in too many instances, inflexible. So the white man has refused to accept the black man as an equal, and the black man has not heretofore had the cultural ethos wherein he could assert himself as a man; thus this lack of freedom has allowed the dehumanizing process to become a permanent part of the white man's mind-set.

Fear, Economic Exploitation, and Moral Commitment

While the basic economic foundations of slavery in colonial America can hardly be overemphasized, human attitudes dictated by ideas (sometimes religious) or fears must not be discounted. From earliest times until even now, two currents of thought appear among whites in America: prejudice and abolitionism. One or the other seems always in focus. While it is true that both these attitudes can be traced in a large part to economic interests (prejudice as a consciously induced means of justifying ruthless economic exploitation, abolitionism or liberalism as a consciously induced means of attacking the dangerous economic competition offered by slavery), both appeared before economic pressures alone could have warranted them.[6]

Prejudice leading to black discrimination has always been partly based on fear. Speaking of why the early American white settlers hated black people, historian Robert Goldston is right when he observes that

feelings of fear, inadequacy, and self-hatred or contempt are often resolved by clinging to derogatory beliefs about others. And the Negro, because of his "high visibility" (easy identification because of color), his utterly foreign cultural background, and his largely unknown place of origin, was the most obvious as well as the safest target for the uneasy settler.[7]

With a ready-made target—the black man—the white man, not far removed from near-slavery in Europe, had an object at which he could direct his insecurity and his frequent lack of confidence in his struggle with the Indians and the natural forces of the new world. This is how much prejudice got started, but later it was legislated and institutionalized by those who stood to gain by it.

Beyond Expediency

Historically, the black man's plight has too often been given attention only when some other, unrelated conditions made it mandatory, when it was politically expedient, or when it was economically prudent to do so. Too few times has the motivation been purely moral; or, at least, too many actions can be attributed to factors that were less than moral or

[6] Goldston, *The Negro Revolution*, p. 44.
[7] *Ibid.*

ethical in motive. Independent conscience has almost always, with too few exceptions, been submerged by interests that were less than moral or ethical. Indeed, few people like to recall the clear words of Abraham Lincoln, stating why he freed the slaves: "My paramount object in this struggle is to save the Union, and is not either to save or destroy slavery. If I could save the Union without freeing any slave, I would do it; and if I could save it by freeing some and leaving others alone, I would also do that." [8]

This is not to contend that Mr. Lincoln, or many others, did not agonize to some degree over the moral implications of slavery; it is not to suggest that there were no strong white protesters against the institution of slavery; it is not to forget that men like Elijah Parish Lovejoy, William Lloyd Garrison, and John Brown were willing to die for the cause of abolition. It is rather to say that the national policy was either politically or economically inspired. Few times have the problems of race received the moral support they deserved, even in modern times. Mr. Lincoln expressed this age-old attitude when he asserted that "this is a people's contest. On the side of the Union it is a struggle . . . to afford all an unfettered start, and a fair chance in the race of life." The attitude of Mr. Lincoln and of many influential Northerners was that the war was being fought to save the Union, to put down a rebellion on the part of "combinations too powerful to be suppressed by the ordinary course of judicial proceedings." In Defense Department records the Civil War is still referred to as the War of the Rebellion.[9] Even the question of whether to employ the

[8] "Reply to Horace Greeley," 1862, in *The American Tradition in Literature*, Vol. 1, rev. S. Bradley, R. C. Beatty, and E. H. Long, eds. (New York: W. W. Norton, 1962), p. 1567.
[9] Goldston, *The Negro Revolution*, pp. 108-9.

free black man as a Union soldier was to be deferred until it was seen that he might well mean the difference between the success or the failure of the Union Army.

Though the laws forbidding slave trade were passed long before 1862, and though the British vessels had captured many ships, it was not until then that Captain Nathaniel Gordon became the first and the last slaver to be hanged for engaging in human cargo. Fear of British intervention on the side of the South was more the reason for the strong argument for federal cooperation in the surpression of the slave trade than many of the moral arguments put forth by the abolitionists.

Almost all the early laws dealing with emancipation were politically inspired, and though there were moral grounds for the Emancipation Proclamation, it was issued because it was a politically prudent thing to do. One wonders whether the Proclamation would have been forthcoming, even from one so morally inclined as was Mr. Lincoln, if it had not been so clearly a political necessity.

Reactions to many of the anti-Negro riots in the early days of Emancipation or Reconstruction were politically inspired, and even the Civil Rights Act of April, 1866, was a political response. The Fourteenth Amendment was politically inspired, and because it was not ratified by many of the Southern states, it became a political tool for the radical Republicans eventually to declare the Southern state governments illegal; and, with the help of the black vote, it also helped the radical Republicans to gain control of the South for their political party.

Pro-freedom decisions were easy for the North and for the Republican Party as long as there was no risk, either politically or economically, but when the army had gone and independent moral decisions were risky, the North as well as the South forgot all the civil rights that black people had acquired during those easy days. As soon as conservative Southerners got themselves together, it was easy for them to gain political control again by terror, murder, and political corruption. It was easy for them to frighten Negroes and radical whites from the use of political power and to rob black men of whatever economic advantages they had won. It was too easy for them "to convince the North that: 1— These events were not happening; 2—They might be happening, but they were justified; 3—They might not be justified, but they were expedient; 4—Expediency would bring profit to the North as well as the South." [10]

After the Dred Scott Decision by the U. S. Supreme Court in 1857, many civil rights laws were passed, even the far-reaching Civil Rights Law of 1866. Many times, however, too few of them were fully enforced in the South or the North because it was not politically prudent to do so. This attitude appears to be a part of the white mentality in many matters that relate to race, for example, the fact that many laws have not been enforced, and that the extension of the full benefits of the American dream to black people has been too long delayed.

Many other examples could be given for the lack of adherence to moral reasons for a realistic approach to the problems of racism in our national life, but these early examples serve to illustrate how freedom for the ex-slave was sort of a "prudent freedom," based on either political or economic expediency rather than on independent conscience. Thus, it is understandable how racism could become institutionalized in American culture.

[10] *Ibid.*, p. 132.

The Post–Civil War Development of the Black Experience Since 1863

In many ways, much of the black experience also took place after the Civil War and the ultimate end of slavery as an institution. After slavery, however, the black experience took on an added survival dimension, which is often misrepresented as indicating a fuller acceptance by the black man of his treatment. As a slave, the black man was much safer, in a sense, than he was after he became emancipated. As a slave, one will recall, he was regarded as mere property, and if he was killed by another, the person who killed him had to answer to the master to whom he belonged. But after he was freed, the black man became fair game for the white man because he was no economic loss to anyone. His death was regarded as resulting in one less problem for the oppressor, especially if he had been guilty of overt protest.

When slavery was abolished in 1863, the black man had already been stripped of his culture and left with this heritage: he was a lowly black man in a white man's world. The systematized racist, sometimes psychotic, propaganda of the white man that harangued about the mental inferiority of the Negro increased in intensity in the late 1800s and early 1900s. The black man was disenfranchised, terrorized, mutilated, and lynched. The black man became every unacceptable, pernicious idea and impulse that the white man's mind wished to project—e.g., the black man was an animal with a tendency to violence and murder, a ravaging sexual impulse, and so on. The white man psychologically needed so deeply for the black man to be shaped in the image of his projected mental sickness that he created a whole new system of organized discrimination, segregation, and exclusion of the black man from the social structure. In the color caste system

29

white people made sure that any wares they dished out to the black man were inferior. Caucasian Americans conditioned the black man to believe deep inside his heart all the many vile things they said about him. They encouraged, and frequently rewarded, behavior and attitudes in blacks that substantiated their worst stereotypes. Black men were happy-go-lucky, lazy, stupid, irresponsible, etc. The mass media disseminated these images with vigor on radio and in the movies, and like unrelenting electric shocks they helped condition the mind of the black man to say, "Yes, I am inferior."

Besides being propagandized that blackness is evil and black people are no good, black men have, in addition, been continually brainwashed that only "white is right." Traditionally, it was the light-skinned black people with straight hair who were allowed to elevate themselves in America. Of course, the white people suggested that such people were better than other blacks because they had much "white blood." And there are still lingering cliques of light-skinned blacks in our communities who reject their darker brothers. Through the years, black men were taught to despise their kinky hair, broad nose, and thick lips. Even black magazines pushed the straightening of hair and bleaching cream as major weapons in the black man's fight for social acceptability and psychological comfort.

The most tragic, yet predictable, part of all this was that the black man came to form his self-image and self-concept on the basis of what white racists prescribed. Therefore, black men and women learned very quickly to hate themselves and one another because they were blacks. And, paradoxically, black men tended to distrust and hate one another more than they did their white oppressors. Today, there is abundant evidence that racism has left almost irreparable scars on the minds of black people that burden them with an unrelenting, painful anxiety that reaches out for a sense of identity and self-esteem. The current black awareness movement is a counter-movement against the seemingly irremediable psychological damages of the black experience.

Today, it is well recognized that the black man's self-concept is partly determined by factors associated with poverty and low economic class status. However, being black in white America has many implications for the ego development of young black children that are not inherent in other lower-class membership. The black child develops in a color caste system and inevitably acquires the negative self-image that is the natural outcome of such a system. Through contacts with institutionalized symbols of caste inferiority (e.g., segregated schools and neighborhoods)—and more indirectly the reactions of his own family—the black child gradually becomes aware of the social and psychological implications of racial membership. He may see himself as an object of scorn and disparagement, unwanted by the white high-status society, and as a being unworthy of love and affection. Since there had been, until of late, few counter-forces working against this negative evaluation of himself, he developed consciously or unconsciously feelings of inferiority and self-doubt.[11]

Studies support the facts that the black child learns self-hatred early in life, and from then on it molds and shapes his entire personality as he interacts with his environment. In the earliest drawings, stories, and dreams of black children there appear many wishes to be white and a rejection of their own color. They usually prefer white dolls and white friends, and they frequently identify themselves as white and show

[11] Lee Rainwaters, "The Crucible of Identity: The Negro Lower Class Family," in *The Negro American,* p. 193. See also pp. 227-53 of the same volume.

a reluctance to admit that they are black. Studies have shown that black youngsters assign less desirable roles and traits to black dolls. One such study reported that black children in their drawings tended to show blacks as small, incomplete people and whites as strong and powerful.

Until the black awareness movement started, one only had to visit Head Start schools and observe three- to five-year olds to see that these children already suffered a damaged self-esteem. One could hear the children shouting at one another in anger, "black pig, dirty nigger," etc. Much of this negative self-image had been passed to them directly by parents who themselves had been conditioned by racism to hate their blackness. And thus there was a vicious circle perpetuated from generation to generation.[12] Much of this has changed with the advent of black awareness and black studies programs.

Sometimes this self-hatred can be quite subtle. Some black people may retreat into their own world and actually be more afraid of success than they are of failure, because too often failure has come to be what they expect. It is all too frequent that black people with ability, intelligence, and talent do not aspire to higher levels because they fear success. Black Americans tend to have lower aspirations and shy away from competition, particularly with white people.[13] One such study showed that even when blacks receive objective evidence of equal intellectual ability in an interracial situation, they typically still feel inadequate and react submissively. This is what the black experience has meant to too many blacks in white America. This is what the black awareness movement is now addressing itself to. There is gradual change for the better.

[12] *Ibid.*, p. 193.
[13] *Ibid.*

As can be seen from the prior discussion, being black in a white man's world has not been an easy task for the black man, during or after slavery. As Frantz Fanon puts it, a rare knowledge of the nature of being does not fully explain what it means to be black in a white world.

Ontology—once it is finally admitted as leaving existence by the wayside—does not permit us to understand the being of the black man. For not only must the black man be black; he must be black in relation to the white man. Some critics will take it on themselves to remind us that this proposition has a converse. I say that this is false. The black man has no ontological resistance in the eyes of the white man.[14]

The problem is that the black man has never been fully recognized. This is the nature of the current struggle.

[14] Frantz Fanon, *Black Skin, White Masks* (New York: Grove Press, 1967), p. 110.

3

THE PRE–CIVIL WAR EXPRESSIONS OF THE CHURCH AND SLAVERY

The Pre–Civil War White Church

So much has been written about the role of the white church as an instrument to help perfect controls over the black man as a slave that it would seem unnecessary to extend this context to give a full and complete historical review of them all. In this context it will suffice to point out that religion was meant to be one of the most favorable means of control. However, contrary to the white man's intent, religious teachings, almost without exception, created within the mind of the slave all the more desire to be free. In his religious teachings, the white man attempted to convince the black man that

whites derived their right to rule over blacks from God. To question this right was to question the will of God and to incur divine wrath. Catechisms for the instruction of slaves in the Christian religion often contained such instructions as:

Q. Who gave you a master and a mistress?
A. God gave them to me.
Q. Who says that you must obey them?
A. God says that I must.[1]

[1] Goldston, *The Negro Revolution*, p. 70.

It is also revealing to note how many religionists defended slavery. (1) In general, those who defended slavery as apologists did so first on morally neutral grounds, contending that slavery could be whatever the master and bondsman made of it. Since every effort was made to evangelize the slaves, to improve their morals, to teach mercy to the master and obedience to the slave, condemnation of the institution as a whole was unnecessary and inappropriate. (2) As these apologetics entered a second stage, slavery was defended as soundly biblical. Richard Furman, South Carolina's leading Baptist clergyman, contended that "the right of holding slaves is clearly established in the Holy Scriptures, both by precept and example. . . . Neither the spirit nor the letter of Scripture demands the abolition of slavery." [2]

(3) A third phase in the apologetic defense of slavery was economic, totally outside the realm of either moral or spiritual concerns. Slaves were mere property, and laws of the transfer, use, and disposal of property were matters of civil, not ecclesiastical, jurisdiction. The slave was a "thing" before he was a person, thus property rights loomed larger than human rights. Slaves were bartered, deeded, auctioned, mortgaged. They were prizes to be given away in contests, stakes to be won or lost in gambling. The market price of slaves, which fluctuated along with that of cotton and tobacco, was discussed in similar terms. While churchmen never wholly accepted this view, the culture they defended did.[3]

(4) Most agreeable to religionists was the final defense of slavery as a positive good. Shifting from the argument based on the slave as property, many religious leaders also acknowledged the slave as a person. Slavery, they then argued, was a

[2] Edwin Scott Gaustad, A *Religious History of America* (New York: Harper, 1966), pp. 186-88.
[3] *Ibid.*, p. 187.

35

boon to the master and bondsman alike. Providence ordained slavery "for the greatest good," argued James Thornwell of Columbia Theological Seminary. "It has been a link in the wondrous chain of Providence. . . . The general operation of the system is kindly and benevolent; it is a real and effective discipline, and without it we are profoundly persuaded that the African race in the midst of us can never be elevated in the scale of being." [4]

The interesting thing was that when there was no strong argument for the moral rightness of slavery, the ecclesiastical institution loomed higher than moral concern. A large segment of institutional Christianity supported slavery because it was to its advantage to do so; yet, there was always a large segment of the church that never accepted slavery, and had it not been for this segment of people, black and white, the independent moral conscience of the nation would have died. The church, as the custodian of the independent conscience of the nation, at times found itself hard put, however, to keep the house of faith from division. Almost every major religious communion divided over the question of slavery.

The spectacle of the house of faith divided in a torn and tortured America brought heavy reproach to religion. On the one hand, the Bible, or the New Testament at least, was used to extoll liberty for all men; yet on the other hand, the Bible, or at least the Old Testament, was used to justify and endorse slavery. For one church, slavery was considered a sin; for another individual church or group of churches, slavery was conceived as a blessing. This minister freed his slaves, while that minister or missionary retained his. Where could people turn for spiritual insight, inspiration, or moral direction? The white church had two voices.

Religious disillusionment penetrated every quarter, but

[4] *Ibid.*, p. 188.

nowhere more deeply than among black people themselves. Religion, as Wendell Phillips observed in 1848, may have, to his mind, been the "most productive, the most efficient, the deepest idea, and the foundation of American thought and institutions"; but to the black man it was confused and hopeless. As a slave or a freed man, the black man suffered one cruel disappointment after another. The best-known of the ex-slave abolitionists, Frederick Douglass, saw little of productivity, efficiency, or depth in America's churches. "Between the Christianity of this land and the Christianity of Christ," he wrote in his autobiography, "I recognize the widest possible difference."

In his autobiography, *Narrative of the life of Frederick Douglass, An American Slave (1845)*, Douglass recalls his longing for freedom.

I have often, in the deep stillness of a summer's Sabbath, stood all alone upon the lofty banks of that noble bay [Chesapeake], and traced, with saddened heart and tearful eye, that countless number of sails moving off to the mighty ocean. The sight of these always affected me powerfully. My thoughts would compel utterance; and there, with no audience but the Almighty, I would pour out my soul's complaint, in my rude way, with an apostrophe to the moving multitude of ships:
"You are loosed from your moorings, and are free; I am fast in my chains, and am a slave! You move merrily before the gentle gale, and I sadly before the bloody whip! . . . O God, save me! God, deliver me! Let me be free! Is there any God? Why am I a slave? . . . Only think of it; one hundred miles straight north, and I am free! Try it? Yes! God helping me, I will. It cannot be that I shall live and die a slave. I will take to the water. This very bay shall yet bear me into freedom.[5]

Why could not the white church have been of more help to a slave in such a time of deep brooding? And yet the white

[5] Benjamin Quarles, ed. (Cambridge, Mass.: Belknap Press, 1969).

church, which imparted to the slave the religion of the oppressor with the subtle intent of control, was never totally successful in the attempt to use religion as a means of subjugation. Indeed, did the white man forget that Christianity had come into being as the religion of the slaves of the Roman Empire? Nearly two thousand years before the cotton kingdom, Christianity had been a revolutionary doctrine, and its tenets had helped to overthrow the ancient empire. Slaves in Dixie were quick to identify themselves with the oppressed Hebrews of old. Nor were the Christian doctrines of equality before God, love of one's fellowmen, and the innate worth of each human soul lost as they fell upon the ears of the black people of the times. The wonder of it all is that the religion derived from the oppressor became, for the black man, a means of hope. Indeed, how could Douglass have survived such deep moments of brooding, cited above, which must have been common to the black experience, had he not been able to talk to God out of the depths of his abiding faith? Contrary to what some have said, a religion derived from the oppressor, augmented by the African strands of religions almost forgotten, brought viable strength to a black people subjected to the ordeals of slavery.

In our times one could not understand the great sin of the white church were it not for such sensitive persons as Kyle Haselden, who reminded his fellow white churchmen that:

We must ask whether our morality is itself immoral, whether our codes of righteousness are, when applied to the Negro, a violation and distortion of the Christian ethic. Do we not judge what is right and what is wrong in racial relationships by righteousness which is itself unrighteous, by codes and creeds which are themselves immoral? [6]

[6] Kyle Haselden, *The Racial Problem in Christian Perspective* (New York: Harper, 1959), p. 48.

Or another equally perceptive critic, Pierre Berton, when he contends that:

In . . . the racial struggle, there is revealed the same pattern of tardiness, apathy, non-commitment, and outright opposition by the church. . . . Indeed, the history of the race struggle in the United States has been to a considerable extent the history of the Protestant rapport with the status quo. From the beginning, it was the Church that put its blessings on slavery and sanctioned a caste system that continues to this day.[7]

In another context, Kyle Haselden points out that "long before the little signs—'White Only' and 'Colored'—appeared in the public utilities they had appeared in the church."

Later there will be a more specific treatment of the weaknesses or failures of the church, both black and white; however, a final word needs to be said of current white churchmen's stance on the question of race. Dr. Cone makes the cogent observation that

today that same Church sets the tone for the present inhumanity to blacks by remaining silent as blacks are killed for wanting to be treated like human beings. Like other segments of this society, the Church emphasizes obedience to the law of the land without asking whether the law is racist in character, or without even questioning the everyday deadly violence which the law enforcer inflicts on blacks in the ghetto.[8]

These have been some of the traditional characteristics of the white church, and it would seem that they reflect how very deep the roots of racism have grown within the life of our culture. It is regrettable that the church did not stand

[7] Pierre Berton, *The Comfortable Pew* (Philadelphia: Lippincott, 1965), pp. 28-29.
[8] Cone, *Black Power and Black Theology*, pp. 74-75.

over against society and assert itself in words and deeds that were more authentically Christian.

The Pre–Civil War Black Church

No other institution growing out of slavery and the confused time of reconstruction has quite equaled the black church. It, and it alone, has stood as a sure bulwark against despair. It has held in common unity more black people than any other institution, and it has had more influence in molding the thoughts and life of black people in America than has any other single agency. In its beginning it was largely a rural institution. Called of God to serve an oppressed, enslaved people, the black church has carried its responsibility in the "heat of the day." The black church took the religion of the oppressor and made of it a tool for the survival of an oppressed people, and this it achieved under the watchful eye of the oppressor. The mobility created by the slave trade, the destruction of the black family, and the prohibition of the African's language served to destroy the social cohesion of the African slave. But for the black church as an institution, and Christianity as a faith, the black man would have soon despaired. As Dr. Cone puts it: "But few slaves committed suicide. Most refused to accept the white master's definition of black humanity and rebelled with every ounce of humanity in them. The black church became the home base for revolution." [9]

The black church was a creation of a black people whose daily existence was filled with encounter after encounter with the extensive dehumanizing and brutalizing reality of slavery. It is no small wonder then that the black church

[9] *Ibid.*, p. 92.

became, for the black man, the one source of personal identity and the sense of community with other slaves. It is strange indeed that the black churchman did not accept the white man's interpretation of Christianity, which suggested that the gospel was concerned with freedom of the soul and not with freedom of the body. But this fact can be attributed to the genius of the black church and its black preacher.

Many have been critical of the black church because of its otherworldly emphasis, but they do not understand that much of the theology of the black church was necessarily of compensatory "content of hope," because slavery under the white oppressor completely destroyed the black people's hopes in this world. It is no small wonder that the spirituals, the songs, and the sermons in the black church reflected so much of hope beyond despair. Indeed, all would have despaired had they not been able to sing: "I's So Glad that Trubbles Don't Last Always," "Soon I Will Be Done with the Trubbles of the World." A large majority of slaves refused to believe that God was irrelevant, but, as they looked at this world, he appeared to offer them little hope. Therefore, to believe, to sustain his hope, the average black man had to look forward to another reality beyond time and space.

This "other world" emphasis by the black church did not mean that black people accepted the view of the white churchmen that God had ordained slavery. It must also be remembered that all the spirituals and sermons were not otherworldly, as some would contend; some had as their central theme the liberation of the slave here in this world. Such spirituals as "Go Down, Moses" give cogent testimony to that fact.

Within this context we must recall that many historic events took place before the birth of the black church. It must be remembered that the black church had its inception after

41

the question arose whether a converted slave had to be freed. Such was the custom during the early days of slavery. Many of the states soon passed laws that permitted black slaves to be retained after conversion. The state of Virginia, one of the first to do so, passed a law in 1667 which set a pattern for the several other colonial states. Subsequent to that time the Bishop of London declared that:

Christianity does not make the least alteration in civil property; that the freedom that Christianity gives, is a freedom from the bondage of sin and Satan, and from the dominion of their lusts and passions and inordinate desires; now as to their outward condition they remain as before, even after baptism.[10]

Three events gave birth and growth to the black church. (1) First of all, there was the increased production of cotton, related to the invention of the cotton gin by Whitney in America, and the invention of the weaving machine in England. (2) The second event was the arrival in America of the evangelical Christian bodies such as the Methodists, Baptists, and Presbyterians. (3) Finally, more than to any other thing, the growth of the black church can be attributed to rise of the black preacher. He was the genius of the black church because he was of the people, he was a symbol for the slave, and usually he was a born leader of men. In fact, at times the preacher was the only leader permitted. His task was to preach to slaves in such a way as not to attack slavery openly, but rather to make of religion, derived from the master oppressor, a means of developing not only an adequate discipline for surviving the ordeals of the black experience, but also a living ground of hope for the future, no matter what the ordeal. Some leaders admonished the people to take up

[10] W. E. B. DuBois, *The Negro Church* (Atlanta: The Atlanta University Press, 1903).

arms, as in the case of Nat Turner; others advised the slaves to make a complete adjustment, as did George Liele; but most of the black preachers worked out a theology of discipline and made of religion a living ground of hope. It was not a passive hope; for most it was not a discipline of adjustment, but an active hope and a viable discipline of protest.

There were at least three types of churches to which black people went. (1) There was the mixed church, with separate seating for blacks. But soon this ended in protests such as the one staged by Richard Allen, who later founded the AME Church. (2) The second type of black church was the separate church under white leadership, white preachers, etc. (3) The third type was the black church under black leadership. During the early days before and even after the Civil War, this type of church was not given too much encouragement by whites, because they feared that it could well become—as it did in many cases—a source of rebellion and protest. After such rebellions as those led by Nat Turner and Denmark Vesey, the separate black church was most carefully watched.

The black church needed watching, if the white man expected the converted and the adherents to Christianity to embrace it and make an adjustment to slavery. It was the black preacher who, more clearly than any other person of his time, articulated the aspirations of a people. The word of the Reverend Highland Garnet illustrates with what eloquence such men communicated the gospel. In 1848, at Buffalo, New York, he said:

The humblest peasant is as free in the sight of God as the proudest monarch that ever swayed a sceptre. Liberty is a spirit sent out from God and, like its great Author, is no respecter of persons.
Brethren, the time has come when you must act for yourselves.

43

It is an old and true saying that, "if hereditary bondmen would be free, they must themselves strike the blow." [11]

It is interesting to note in this context that theologically most black preachers, as well as many whites, could not reconcile a just God with slavery. They did not, with few exceptions, take part in revolts, yet they were collective in their contention that God could not condone slavery and be adjudged a just God. The black man could not embrace a God whom he conceived as being just and at the same time accept slavery as ordained by him. The great problem was to see God as belonging to both slave and master. To reconcile God as being related to the oppressor and, while not approving of his deeds, even loving him is a hard thing even for many modern theological thinkers. Is this not the reason many theologians tend to call equate God with the good people? Is this not why they tend to call his wrath down upon the unjust or the enemy? Is it any wonder that the black preacher mused over the question of why? The Reverend Mr. Nathaniel Paul asked in such a mood of musing:

Tell me, ye mighty waters, why did ye sustain the ponderous load of misery? Or speak, ye winds, and say why it was that ye executed your office to waft them onward to the still more dismal state; and ye proud waves, why did you refuse to lend your aid and to have overwhelmed them with your billows? Then should they have slept sweetly in the bosom of the great deep, and so have been hid from sorrow. And, oh thou immaculate God, be not angry with us, while we come into this thy sanctuary, and make bold inquiry in this thy holy temple, why it was that thou didst look on with the calm indifference of an unconcerned spectator, when thy holy law was violated, thy divine authority

[11] Quoted in Benjamin E. Mays, *The Negro's God* (New York: Atheneum, 1968), p. 46.

44

despised and a portion of thine own creatures reduced to a state of mere vassalage and misery.[12]

To muse thus, to agonize thus, and then to find an answer within himself was the genius of the black preacher; for such must have been the thoughts of many of the early slaves and later freed men who looked to him for an answer to their deep agony of heart and soul. Mr. Paul gives eloquent answer in these further words of musing:

Hark! While he answers from on high: hear Him proclaiming from the skies—Be still, and know that I am God! Clouds and darkness are around about me; yet righteousness and judgment are the habitation of my throne. I do my will and pleasure in the heavens above, and in the earth beneath; it is my sovereign prerogative to bring good out of evil, and cause the wrath of man to praise me, and the remainder of that wrath I will restrain.[13]

"How long, Lord?" may well have been the question from many lips, and probably no other person caught up an answer in words quite as did Bishop Daniel Payne of the AME Church when he said:

"With God one day is a thousand years and a thousand years as one day. Trust in him, and he will bring slavery and all of its outrages to an end." These words from the spirit world acted on my troubled soul like water on a burning fire, and my aching heart was soothed and relieved from its burden of woes.[14]

Hope, then, for the black slave preacher was a kind of restless protest. On the surface, it seemed patient, but it was rather a deep, restless kind of calmness that would not be

[12] *Ibid.*, pp. 43-44.
[13] *Ibid.*, p. 44.
[14] *Ibid.*, p. 49.

stilled. This is what Jürgen Moltmann means when he asserts that to have hope is "not only a consolation in suffering, but also the protest of divine promise *against* suffering." [15] He rightly asserts that for the Christian to be sustained in hope in times of great stress, he must be assured that God is fighting against it.

It is strange that this section should close on a note from one of the great white theologians of hope, and that his voice is heard in our times.The black slave preacher's emphasis on hope was just as clear as Moltmann's, only more relevant for his times than many have found Moltmann's thought for his times. The black preacher taught his people to look to the future, to visualize a new day. For the black preacher, religion was a part of social justice in this world. Joseph Washington was in error to contend that the black slave preacher was, because of his lack of formal theological training, theologically illiterate. Rather, he was a great theologian to have been able to communicate God's message of hope at a time of great despair.[16] To preach to a people enslaved would have been task enough, but to communicate hope was a theological contribution matched by only the prophets of old.

[15] *Theology of Hope*, p. 21.
[16] See Dr. Washington's *Black Religion* (Boston: Beacon Press, 1964) for a full treatment of this subject.

4

POST–CIVIL WAR EXPRESSIONS OF THE CHURCH

The Post–Civil War White Church

One of the most fruitful sources of self-deception in the church is the proclamation of great ideals and principles without any clue to their relation to the controversial issues of the day.[1] This idea of Reinhold Niebuhr, taken from his *Leaves from the Notebook of a Tamed Cynic*, 1929, gives some testimony to the plight of the white church in Post–Civil War America. These were difficult times for the white church. It had proclaimed a gospel to the slaves; they had taken it and made of it a religion of liberation. Now white people were to try to find a Christian way to live with a people who had once been slaves, still adjudged by some as subhuman, and by all, with few exceptions, to be yet inferior. How should the church react to such a people? For the most part, the white church remained silent on many critical issues concerning race relations, and it thus helped to create an ethos that was further dehumanizing to black people in America. Gunnar Myrdal cites many preachers who were very active in reviving

[1] See Gaustad's *Religious History of America*.

47

the Ku Klux Klan after the First World War, and indeed
he was right when he wrote that there is little question that
the church became closely identified with the social context
in which it lived.[2] Haselden further writes:

So far as the major denominations are concerned, it is the
story of indifference, vacillation, and duplicity. . . . It is a history
in which the church not only compromised its ethic to the mood
and practice of the times but was itself actively unethical,
sanctioning the enslavement of human beings, producing the
patterns of segregation, urging upon the oppressed Negro the
extracted sedatives of the Gospel, and promulgating a doctrine
of interracial morality which is itself immoral.[3]

Late in the eighteenth century, the Reverend Thomas
Bacon summed it up in a letter to his sponsoring mission
society in England: "Religion among us seems to wear the
face of the country; part moderately cultivated, the greatest
part, wild and savage." Has this too often characterized Christianity? Has it radically changed conditions rather than itself
make the radical adjustment to its social context? Almost
without exception, the white church has done the latter.

Dr. Cone best characterizes the white churchmen's problem when he writes:

The moral and religious implications of any act of risk are always
sufficiently cloudy to make it impossible to be certain of right
action. Because man is finite, he can never reach that state of
security in which he is free of anxiety when he makes moral
decisions. This allows the irresponsible religious man to grasp
a false kind of religion and political security by equating law and

[2] Gunnar Myrdal, *An American Dilemma: The Negro Problem and
Modern Democracy* (New York: Harper, 1947), p. 860.

[3] Haselden, *The Racial Problem in Christian Perspective*, p. 63.

48

order with Christian morality. If someone calls his attention to the inhumanity of the political system toward others, he can always explain his loyalty to the state by suggesting that this system is the least evil of any other existing political state. He can also point to the lack of clarity regarding the issues, whether they concern race relations or the war in Vietnam. This will enable him to compartmentalize the various segments of the societal powers so that he can rely on other disciplines to give the word on the appropriate course of action. This seems to characterize the style of many religious thinkers as they respond to the race problem in America.

Therefore, it is not surprising that the sickness of the Church in America is also found in the main stream of American religious thought.[4]

One probably finds another explanation equally as interesting, and indeed more novel, in the explanation offered by Geddes Hanson when he contends that:

The ability of the traditional church to relate the corpus of its theology to what I have described as the self-consciously black experience is inhibited by the fact that it brought a post-Constantinian experience to the task of theologizing. Prior to Emperor Constantine's confession the church was a group of people hunted, hounded, and harassed. It is natural to assume that the concerns and perspectives that were dominant within this community—which was having its own "black" experience —were quite different from those which became dominant as the faith assumed its new role as the cohesive force within the Roman Empire. Christian theologizing that would have developed apart from the Constantinian confession would have been quite different, both in the categories with which it dealt and in the content of those categories, from that to which we have fallen heir. I am convinced that in both category and content the non-Constantinian theology would have avoided the hang-ups and limitation of scope inherent in the post-Constantinian process.

The crux of the matter is the position of privilege into which

[4] Cone, *Black Theology and Black Power*, pp. 82-83.

the church was catapulted. Because it was no longer hunted, hounded, and harassed, there were those aspects of life which were no longer of as pressing a concern as they might have been. Because of a position in which it shared the power and enjoyed the protection of the Empire, the church became very conservative in its outlook. Its concern was with those themes whose development promised a peaceful, orderly enhancing of the status of the government to which it owed its emancipation. The themes of love, charity, joy, peace, evangelism, purity, legality became dominant. Rightful affiliation and doctrinal purity became pressing concerns.

In becoming the lapdog of the empirial society the church could not expediently pursue those matters which press upon deprived, powerless people. The matter of power, for instance, became the concern of the temporal authority and a recessive theme in theology, despite the fact that it is a theme within the context of which the Bible explores the work of Christ. The concept of conflict and its management was lost as a subject for suitable exploration by a church concerned to keep peace in the Empire. An examination of the revolutionary nature of what God was doing in Jesus Christ took back seat to the now very familiar determination to bulwark the status quo by hedging change around with procedures, laws, orderliness, and decency. It was natural that a fellowship of privileged persons who would depend upon a "secular" agency to bear arms in active defense of its best interests would be less inclined to deal critically with the "fire and sword" theme in the gospel than to foster an uncritical development of the theme of nonviolence.[5]

If one can accept the Hanson criticisms, somewhat akin to similar arguments offered by Gibson Winter in his critique of the modern church, he can conclude also with the contentions of Dr. Cone that

it is time for theology to make a radical break with the world by seeking to bring to the problem of color the revolutionary implications of the gospel of Christ. It is time for theology to

[5] Hanson, "Black Theology and Protestant Thought," pp. 5 ff.

leave its ivory tower and join the real issues, which deal with the dehumanization of blacks in America. It is time for theologians to relate their work to life-and-death issues, and in so doing to execute its function of bringing the church to a recognition of its task in the world.[*]

In reading the history of the white church just after the Civil War and subsequent to that time, including the critical days of reconstruction, one might well conclude by pointing out that two grave errors were made which constituted the greatest failures of the post–Civil War white church. First of all, most of the major denominations separated themselves from the black churchmen either by involuntary or by voluntary agreement. By and large, this separation meant that they adopted a kind of condescending, missionary, paternalistic relationship with black people which, except for an occasional concern, left the newly freed slave to shift for himself. This does not discount the fact that there were those denominations which did establish means of education and evangelism for the newly freed slave. However, as good as these actions were, they did not take seriously the full concept of equality under God. Second, by not facing squarely the question of equality under God, the post–Civil War white church soon found itself having to help further justify inequality. Here one recalls the counsel of theologian L. Harold DeWolf when he advised that "the best time to face evil is at the point of the first encounter, without a direct, precise, resolute confrontation at the first encounter." DeWolf contends that otherwise one will find that evil has grown in strength while he himself is weaker.

Had the early post–Civil War white church exemplified more than mere passive concern that the newly freed black

[*] *Black Theology and Black Power*, p. 83.

man suffered discrimination, disfranchisement, and death by the lynch mobs, it would probably have had more influence even until now. By remaining silent, passive, and inactive, the white church found itself, even after slavery, having to rationalize the lynch mobs and even the Klan. Much of its theology was to become a theology of segregation. By not confronting the evil—racism—as it revealed itself in new forms and in new structures, the post–Civil War white church soon found that the enemy, even if it had conceived it so, had soon grown too strong. Not too much later historically, the white church became a part of the system, fully sharing in its benefits.

The Post–Civil War Black Church

Dr. Cone, in his book *Black Theology and Black Power*, and Dr. Washington, in his book *Black Religion*, are almost one in their contention that the post–Civil War period saw a marked change in the black church. The black church, many times still an "invisible institution" during slavery, now became visible as an institutional entity, uniting in spirit to give larger expression to the quest for black independence. Indeed, the black church was a means of expressing freedom. According to Mays and Nicholson, new churches sprang up everywhere—some organized by black groups themselves, others as a result of direct expulsion from white congregations and denominations, where converted slaves had been members.[7] Dr. Cone may well be only partly right in pointing out that

it is a credit to the humanity of black people that they recognized their presence in white services as an adjunct of slavery. Therefore, many of them left before being expelled. For this reason,

[7] See *The Negro's Church*.

we may describe the black churches during this period as a place of retreat from the dehumanizing forces of white power. It was one place in which the blacks were "safe" from the new racist structures that replaced slavery. The black church gradually became an instrument of escape instead of, as formerly, an instrument of protest.[8]

The black church, Dr. Cone further contends, "lost its zeal for freedom in the midst of new structures of the post-reconstruction period." The black minister remained the spokesman for the black people, but, faced with insurmountable obstacles, he succumbed to the cajolery and the bribery of the white power structure and became its foil.[9]

Dr. Cone further contends that for freedom, he substituted drinking, dancing, and smoking; and this-world concerns were minimized in favor of a kingdom beyond this world. Endurance now, liberty later was the general theme of the black church.

After such sweeping criticism of the black church and of the black minister, Dr. Cone comes back and rightly retracts or modifies his statements to concede that

in all fairness to the black church and its leaders, it should be pointed out that the apostasy of the black church is partly understandable. If they had not supported the caste system of segregation and discrimination, they would have placed their lives and the lives of their people in danger. They would have been lynched and their churches burned. Thus, by cooperating with the system, they protected their lives, and the lives of their people from the menacing threat of racism. But this is not an excuse for their lack of obedience to Christ. It merely explains it.[10]

[8] *Black Theology and Black Power,* p. 104.
[9] *Ibid.,* p. 105.
[10] *Ibid.,* p. 107.

Dr. Cone, had he fixed on this latter explanation, could well have asked himself more questions about the cultural ethos of the difficult times in which these men lived and served. It is quite easy to say what one should have done had one's life and the life of one's whole people been at stake. A part of the genius of the black church is that it carefully guided a people through a time of great danger. To preach a full truth, not to compromise at points, might well have invited genocide. Post–Civil War times called for great caution; the climate was not nearly so permissive for black church life as in pre–Civil War times. Newly freed black men had been put in places of leadership, displacing whites. Many times they had been removed from such places by force; many times they had been killed in the process. Law and order was for the white man. The death of a slave represented a loss to the owner, but a freed dead black man was no loss to anyone, as has been pointed out earlier. Whether one is critical of the black church for its lack of aggressive protest, or rather praises it for its strategy of deception, which surely saved a people, may be determined by how one reads post–Civil War history.

Indeed, it is hard to read objectively the history of the post–Civil War black church and come to an absolute conclusion that "the real sin of the black church and its leaders is that they even convinced themselves that they were doing the right thing by advocating the obedience to white oppression as a means of entering at death the future age of heavenly bliss." [11] It is true that this was but a part of the Christian ethic, which may have been common to much of the ethic of the white church, but such a facet of the total ethic could well have come from the common use of the Bible. To in-

[11] *Ibid.*

ternalize such an ethic may well have furnished the moral strength needed to withstand the further disappointment of having freedom extended by a government and then seeing that same government side with the oppressor to withdraw that freedom bit by bit. Having conceded as much, however, one does not conclude that such an emphasis was the total gospel of the black church.

A careful reading of Bennett's *Before the Mayflower* does not lead one to conclude that the black preacher or the black church did not play an important part in sustaining a people in deep and troubled times. It is of interest to note, with Bennett, that the years between 1867 and 1877 were strange years of black reconstruction. Dr. DuBois called them the "mystic years," the years when, "intoxicated perhaps by the emotional bang of the big war, taunted by the arrogance of the conquered South, spurred on by economic and political forces, the North took the longest stride America has ever taken: it decided to try democracy." [12] Many ministers turned to politics and became some of the strong leaders of the period; churches were the meeting places. In addition they became educational institutions, and were supportive of all the aspirations of the people. Carter G. Woodson points out that

there were during the Reconstruction period, moreover, so many other necessities with which the Negroes had to be supplied that the Negro preacher, often the only one in a community usually sufficiently well developed to lead the people, had to devote his time not only to church work but to every matter of concern to the race.[13]

[12] Lerone Bennett, *Before the Mayflower: A History of the Negro in America* (Baltimore: Penguin Books, 1966), p. 186.

[13] Woodson, *The History of the Negro Church* (New York: The Associated Publisher, 1921), pp. 220-21.

That these were difficult times for the black man is summed up by Sterling Tucker in his book *Beyond the Burning,* in which he points out that

during the slavery period, there was no freedom, no opportunity at all. When the civil war ended and the slaves were freed, the country acted as though it had purged itself of all guilt. That the whites had loosened black chains was a selfless and benevolent act. And there began and ended their responsibility. Hence, the black man was left free to deal with starvation, poverty and want, for there was little, if any opportunity afforded him.[14]

The newly freed black man became the political tool of the radical facet of the Republican Party during this ten-year period, but when the southern white man declared war and vowed to recapture his place of advantage at all cost—meaning taking the life of every black man, woman, and child— the government merely turned its head and let the process continue until a new type of enslavement materialized. Bennett further contends that the black man was freer in slavery than he was in post–Civil War America, especially after 1877.[15] The black man was freed for awhile only to be re-enslaved.

[14] Tucker, *Beyond the Burning* (New York: Association Press, 1968). p. 45.
[15] See Chapter VIII in Bennett's *Before the Mayflower* for an interesting treatment of "Black Power in Dixie," pp. 183 ff.

5

THE NATURE OF THE CHURCH IN BLACK THEOLOGICAL PERSPECTIVE

Most white and black persons who criticize the church and its actions do so from a frame of reference that seems to suggest that they make the following basic assumptions. First, they seem to think that the church, as congregation, as community, as ecclesia, is something that is formed and founded once and for all and remains constant and unchanged. They do not theologically conceive of the church as being the actual process of a congregating community; thus, they miss the fact that the people of God become an ecclesia only by the fact of a repeated concrete event when God meets them there. Congregation, community, and church are not mutually exclusive terms, but should be seen as interconnected. In this sense, then, each time the people of God come together as a congregating community, the occasion of their gathering has the potential of becoming the "event church," provided the people gathered lay hold on the conceptualized meaning of the entire promise of the gospel, become aware of the availability of the undivided grace of the Father, and are made fully conscious of the abiding presence of the undivided Christ.

If the church is really the people of God, then it is impossible to see it as something set apart from everything earthly, from error and sin. This would be an *idealizing misconception* of the Church, by which it would become an unreal, distant ideal surrounded by a false halo, rather than a real historical church. Such an ideal Church would have no faults or blemishes, would know nothing of error and sin, and so would need no repentance and penance.[1]

Better understood then, the event church, the "true church," is only an occasional full realization, because it comes into focus only when the conditions are right for the people of God gathered.

Second, it would seem that those who are critical of the church are also critical of the whole of its functional potential in the light of one error, fault, or sin. This tendency rules out the fact that an imperfect people of God may well come together in the name of Christ, in the hope of receiving God's undivided grace with the entire promise of the gospel, and while gathered become an event church as a result of something heard, something done, or something mutually shared. They may have sensed something that made them aware that God was there. It would seem, from such a conclusion, that the event church is not a sustained entity in focus at all times. The true church, according to this definition, is best characterized as a group of people called of God to be the church in the world and, accepting such a calling, gathered as people of God in his name. But they experience the "event status" only at rare moments in the experience of their gathering. Though on every occasion of their gathering they are called of God to become the event church, they only occasionally achieve the status of being the church.

[1] Hans Küng, *The Church* (New York: Sheed & Ward, 1967), p. 131.

Beyond the church gathered or even the event church, the people of God are called to be the church in but not of the world in both word and deed. They can do no other. Both the black and the white post–Civil War churches failed, in degrees and on many occasions, to become adequate instruments of God's calling to be servant. First, as has been mentioned before, the white church allowed itself to become a tool of the cultural ethos; its theology attempted to justify slavery and to convert the black man to a belief that he was not equal to his white brother under God. The white post–Civil War church gave itself to the aid of the dehumanizing process before and after slavery because it too allowed itself to become too much at one with racism. Second, the white church allowed its beliefs about man to become eroded so much with the idea that "white is right" that whiteness became a part of the creedal stance of the white church. Racism became a part of the white "Christian" man's way of life, and whiteness as an attitude was thus internalized to such an extent that it did not have to be taught. Third, the white post–Civil War church allowed itself to enjoy the economic advantages of the cultural ethos so much that there was a blending of the physical with the spiritual. The physical and the spiritual ideas soon became coextensive one with the other to the extent that separation became almost impossible. Becoming so infused with racism, the white church could not transcend its human limitations, its cultural context, to become at one with the ideal of the family of God, or with the concept of God as Father of all mankind. Somewhere along the way the "brothers in Christ" idea became a substitute. Indeed, a spiritual brotherhood could accommodate the underlying idea of inequality. The brothers in Christ concept was not a problem, but "brotherhood" within the context of the "family of God" did offer a "one blood" problem.

Just to illustrate the problem, on all questions of race or at any point where race was involved, the white church could not act in keeping with the high and simple ideal of just affording the black man the respect due another human being. He was rather treated as a "black person," and any response to him was at this lesser level. So that on matters of racism—at worship, at study, in fellowship, in all matters of blood brotherhood—the white people of God gathered could have little hope of becoming the event church. Indeed, how often was the call of God heard and the "white people of God" congregated, and just one little mention of race kept them from achieving the high calling to become on that occasion, by act, deed, attitude, thought, or aspiration, the event church!

The black post–Civil War church was not without its moments and occasions of sin. The ethos of the times presented a different set of circumstances for the black church. It was poor; very often it became an object of paternalism and charity. But too often, to become such an object, it had to compromise both belief and action. Had it maintained its freedom, the black church could have counted many more of the wrongs of racism that were accepted without question. Indeed, the first ten years, 1867 to 1877, both churches had an ample start. Lerone Bennett furnishes insight into those "mystic years" by pointing out that

Negroes and whites were going to school together, riding on street cars together and cohabiting, in and out of wedlock (Negro men were marrying white women in the South, but it was more fashionable, investigators reported, for white men to marry Negro women). An interracial board was running the University of South Carolina where a Negro professor, Richard T. Greener, was teaching white and black youth metaphysics and logic.

These things were happening on the higher levels. What of the masses? How was it with them? They were struggling, as they had always struggled, with the stubborn and recalcitrant earth. But there was a difference. Now there was hope. Never before— never since—has there been so much hope. A black mother knew that her boy could become governor. The evidence of things seen, the evidence of things heard fired millions of hearts. Black mothers walked ten, fifteen and twenty miles to put their children in school. They sacrificed and stinted. They bowed down and worshipped the miraculous ABC's from whom so many blessings flowed. . . . Was it not clear that a black boy could go as far as nerve, energy and ability would carry him? Black mothers, bending over washtubs, could hope. Black boys, in cotton fields, could dream.[2]

The great sin of both the black and white post–Civil War churches was that they did not keep alive such a hope. The greater sin was to become a part, each in its own way, of the re-enslavement process. To fix on one of the many examples, as an illustration, the whole concept of inferiority did not become so completely infused within the cultural ethos until post–Civil War times. To be sure, there were arguments during slavery, but they did not become life-and-death issues for the white man until his position of economic, political, and social advantage was threatened by the newly freed black man. It was subsequent to this period that he took many more pains to exclude from history the black man's past, it was during these times that he strove systematically to develop the myth of the black man's degraded, savage bestiality. Not only was the black man taught that he was culture-less, a Black Adam in a new garden, but there was an added attempt to convince him that he was doubly fortunate in being rescued from naked barbarism and simultaneously clothed with a superior culture. So compelling was this myth,

[2] Bennett, *Before the Mayflower*, p. 184.

so lacking of any persuasive evidence to the contrary, so universally prevalent the stereotypes of Afro-Americans in their American world that until very recently black people adopted them unquestioningly themselves. Even such black historians of note as Carter G. Woodson and W. E. B. DuBois were among those who supported such a questionable myth.[3]

By accepting much of the literature of the white religious publishing houses, by accepting money and counsel, by accepting schools set up by the white man, by accepting textbooks written by him, and by acquiring gradually a deep expressed and unexpressed yearning to be accepted by the oppressor, the black man, in all his institutions, including the church, lost the will to be black. He rather yearned to become white.

Yet, it is hard to realize that the black church, if it took seriously its task as educator, would not have had trouble with the Fatherhood of God concept, except that the concept of God, for the black church, transcended color. Not one spiritual would suggest that color or equality would be a problem "over Jordan." It would seem that this is the one place where the black man knew he was equal—in Heaven. He could not say it, at times, but there seemed always a reserve.

[3] See A. Philip Randolph, Education Fund Booklet 6: *Black Studies*, pp. 20 ff.

6

THE MEANING OF THE CURRENT BLACK AWARENESS MOVEMENT

The Courage to Be Black

A part of the black man's identity problem lies in the fact that he has not been too sure who he was at any given moment in the context of American culture. As has already been cited, when he was brought to this country and subjected to the black experience, a part of the aim of the dehumanizing process was to strip him of his original sense of personhood. To make him a fit slave, his sense of an African heritage had to be erased from both the conscious and subconscious minds. Group as well as individual freedom was taken away, and any semblance of authority, as may have been derived from his sense of independent personhood or groupness, had to be erased. Any sense of authority which the slave may have had was to be derived only from his master, and his self-identity was to be related to that of his master. Any authority such as was assumed by men like Nat Turner, Denmark Vesey, and others was suppressed. Quick examples were made of all black men who did not submit to the complete will of the master.

The black man in a strange land, cut off from his proud

heritage, which had been a part of both his conscious and unconscious mind-set, soon became confused as to who he was. Since he could not assert himself in the pure essence of his true selfhood, he was never sure of himself in relation to his master. He bore no name of his own; he had acquired the name of his master. Without a clear native cultural identity, without a clear native religious identity, and without the freedom of an independent authority, collective or individual, the black man soon lost his true sense of any authority. Thus, he always asserted a kind of pseudo-personhood or identity which was not black, because he had long since lost the courage to assert a bold black personhood. His will to survive the black experience forced him to practice the art of deception; he knew to assert a bold black selfhood, comparable to what the Indian did in asserting a red personhood, would be fatal. On the other hand, there was also the frustration inherent in his subconscious wish to assert a white selfhood after the image of his master. However, because psychologically or physically the black man could never be transformed into such a being, he has always had an ontological problem in the lack of the courage to be black. To add to the frustration, people of slightly lighter shades of color seem to have been rewarded even by people of their same group. In yesteryears it paid in many many different ways not to be black. It surely paid not to assert blackness. Now comes the black awareness movement and its emphasis on blackness. What does it mean?

The current movement toward black awareness merely means that the black man has come to a point in history where he is both willing and free to assert his right to self-determination, to possess racial pride, and to engage in the pursuit of blackness.

It is important that the movement toward black awareness

has come to the black community at such a time in history because we may now better understand what Dr. DuBois meant when he tried to delineate the role of the newly emancipated black man in America, which the black man of that time neither accepted nor fully understood. How much better off would he have been had he understood Dr. DuBois, who wrote of the black man in 1903:

One feels his two-ness—an American Negro, two souls, two thoughts, two unreconciled strivings, two warring ideals, in one dark body. . . .
The history of the American Negro is the history of this strife —this longing to attain self-conscious manhood, to merge his double self into a better and truer self. . . . He would not Africanize America, for America has too much to teach the world and Africa. He would not bleach the Negro soul in a flood of white Americanism, for he knows that Negro blood has a message for the world. He simply wishes to make it possible for a man to be both a Negro and an American without being cursed and spit upon.[1]

While seeming to forget this problem, the black man accepted another premise, a false one, an idea that he could become not only acceptable as he was, but that he could become, in a sense, white. Herein lies his current frustration. What has been said to the black man throughout this century, by too many of his leaders and by too many white liberals, is that he must think of himself as an individual and not as a member of a group; that if, as an individual, he gained education and money he would first be acculturated and then assimilated into a pluralistic, multiracial society wherein his race would not make any real difference. He

[1] Quoted by James Farmer, "White Liberals and Black Liberations," in *Is Anybody Listening to Black America?* ed. C. Eric Lincoln (New York: Seabury Press, 1968).

would become, in reality, a man in a pluralistic, color-blind community. Men of goodwill, black and white, thought such to be possible. They believed that if assimilation were achieved, both black men and white men as such would lose their racial identity; they both would acquire a human identity that would transcend all ethnic or racial identity. The black man's dilemma, so well delineated by DuBois, was soon forgotten in a new and seemingly impossible hope for a pluralism that has not materialized. And now comes the surge of black awareness. What does it mean? What are some of its deeper ontological implications? What ought it to mean to Christians?

We face a theological question when we ask what message does the church have for a black man who, in such a state of frustration, feels that he must effect some sort of separation from his white brother in order to find himself in his blackness. This is a kind of brokenness which must be related to theology; the problems of self-identity are basically theological.

The Current Meaning of Black Self-assertion

First of all, fundamental to all the deeper questions of black awareness is the more basic question of personhood or being. To what kind of self-identity does black consciousness call a black man? Is the new birth into blackness to be accepted as an end in itself? Is the mere acceptance of one's blackness enough? Does the mere acceptance of one's blackness give a full and complete enough justification for one's existence? Is it not possible to achieve power, "black power," without acquiring an authentic black self-identity? Is it not true that, as a black man, a person may well possess power enough to make others notice him in any important context without the consciousness of a true and authentic self-identity? Indeed, is black self-identity all?

There are many answers to the question of self-identity that are surely inadequate if the black awareness movement is to stand the test of history. It is not enough to wear the dashikis, the Afro or the Natural. Something more is needed. And yet many seem to think that unless one wears these as symbols, he has nothing to contribute to the movement of black awareness. But our concerns with the concept of black awareness must be much deeper than mere visible symbols; they must be related to the very nature of being itself. If this is not what the struggle is about, it may be that we need to reassess its purpose.

The primary question of what it means to have the courage to be a black man within the context of a pro-white culture poses a much deeper theological question when related to the black man's current quest for self-identity. As was suggested above by Dr. DuBois, sometimes the black man has had a serious problem with himself—at times consciously, at other times at a level deeper than consciousness itself. Perhaps the question is best posed: What does it mean to be a man among men? When the question is asked in this light, its implications go to the very roots of the self-identity struggle. Being itself is related to this special question—that its, being under God.

One of the new and most hopeful facets of the current black awareness movement is its accent on the worth of blackness. Just this emphasis alone has tended to change the attitudes and lives of many people within the context of the black community. However, there are still several weaknesses that need to be fully recognized if the movement is to survive the test of history.

The quest for a usable "black self-identity is, as has already been stated, an ontological question that must be answered clearly and precisely. Such an answer must deal with the basic and persistant question of what kind of personhood is being sought by the black man. The kind of personhood or self-identity which is sought is as theologically important as the seeking itself. The problem of authentic selfhood can be seen in at least two different ways. First, as a negative assertion, it can be a mere indication of a deep insecurity. This lack of security can be seen in the pseudo-superior self-identity sought and held by the white supremist, who has always thought himself, because of color alone, to be better than his black brother. Insecure in his whiteness, he asserted an exaggerated personhood to counter a potential black personhood, which he has traditionally refused to accept or to recognize. Indeed, much of the current white mind-set, with few exceptions, still refuses fully to accept black manhood, even today. It has to be forced upon the white mind. So merely to assert a black self-identity to counter a white self-identity, which has traditionally refused to reciprocate, is not enough in the black man's current quest for a usable black self-identity.

To say that I am a man among men, it would seem, means infinitely more than merely to say that I am a black man or a white man. To be black or to be white is merely incidental; but to assert that "I am a man" is essential. Second, another part of the black man's ontological problem lies at the point of projecting any kind of personhood which must be respected, as such, in the context of pro-white American society. Those who would assert a mere black personhood may well run the risk, in white America, of having that black personhood finally accepted, but with the stigma of color still attached, thus, making it still mean or connote less than white personhood. The third ontological question that needs to be raised in this context is, What does it mean to assert oneself in any ontological sense? We have already asserted that in no sense could a slave assert a true selfhood. So is it not also difficult for a person to be clear in his self-perception who cannot assert a personhood that must be accepted as a fact by all with whom he has a social encounter? There are many ways to selfhood being suggested to the black man today as avenues leading to the achievement of an ultimate authentic black self-identity. Many of these ways may well be false. It might help us keep a clear perspective if we looked at some of them in the light of the black man's search for true identity.

Separatism

There are those who contend that the black man will never find his true self-identity within the context of, or in relation to, the white man, whom he blames for so much of his current confusion and frustrations. So, they say, he will have to withdraw psychologically, physically, and socially; only in this apartness will he be able to find the time for adequate self-assessment, and out of such a deep quest will come a concept of true self-identity. In such separation, they contend that there must be studies of Afro-American history, African culture, and American black history, to the end of true self-knowledge, a sense of worth, self-esteem, and an at-homeness with himself. There in apartness, they further contend, the black man will free himself from all that disdains blackness; he will no longer be confused with a desired white identity that he can never quite attain.

However, if we accept the basic belief that authentic selfhood is achieved only in a total community of selves, what does this do with any self-identity achieved in a context less than multiracial? Is it possible to achieve adequate self-identity apart from the total life situation? One wonders if this much separation within the context of our culture is possible anyway.

One might also ask the much deeper question whether separation—no matter what the reason might be—will do any more for the black man than other, older forms of segregation did for him. What, essentially, is the difference between separation for black awareness and separation that was forced? Does separation by force do more harm than separation by choice?

In his letter of resignation from the Board of Directors of Antioch College, Kenneth B. Clark puts an answer this way: "There is absolutely no evidence to support the contention that the inherent damage to human beings of primitive exclusion on the basis of race is any less damaging when demanded or enforced by the previous victims than when imposed by the dominant group." [2]

The question still remains, what are the psychological and theological implications of such a question? If true personhood is achieved out of the matrix of the total context of the group, both secondary and primary, then the question is, Does not separation for any reason make for a kind of incompleteness of personhood? Since collective personhood and the true humanness of the group contribute to the making of individual personhood, is it at all possible for a black man to become truly man within a social matrix that is only black and therefore separate and apart? This is an ontological question that goes deeper than some of the current reasons

[2] This quotation was taken from Dr. Clark's letter of resignation from the Board of Directors of Antioch College when the college made the decision to set up a separate all-Negro Black Studies Institute.

for separation would suggest. As has been cited above, it is of interest that the church, especially the black church, has not addressed itself to this problem sooner. If separation is an interim strategy through which the black community experiences its own integrity, if it is a strategic retreat, how far will it go in its attempt to reshape the image of the black man, and what kind of image will this black image be beyond separation? Who will say when separation is no longer needed?

Most reasoned thinkers would conclude that separation, whether as an interim strategy or as a permanent separatist policy, would but serve to reinforce the black man's inability to compete with the white man for the real power of the real world.

Black Self-affirmation

Never before in the history of the black-white relation in America has the white man felt the full weight of blackness quite so heavy as he is feeling it now. This is so because there is a new identity dimension in the black person who is now asserting himself. Black awareness has become a reality and a new hope within the black community. Black awareness is somewhat analogous to Albert Camus's rebel who says "no" and "yes." He says "no" to conditions which he considers intolerable, and "yes" to that "something in him which 'is worthwhile . . .' and which must be taken into consideration." [3] Because of the new boldness with which the black man is asserting himself, his "no" may well mean that death is more preferable than life, if he is resisted and if his per-

[3] Albert Camus, *The Rebel*, trans. Anthony Bower (New York: Random House, 1956), p. 13.

sonhood is not fully recognized—especially if the latter means that he is not free to be black and at the same time enjoy the fullness of the fruits of freedom. Too many black people are now asserting that it is "better to die on one's feet than to live on one's knees." [4] This is what Paul Tillich is saying in his book *The Courage to Be,* when he points out that "the courage to be is the ethical act in which man affirms his being in spite of those elements of his existence which conflict with his essential self-affirmation." [5] The black man is saying, as he has never quite said before, that "I shall affirm my being, that being is black, and that black being must be recognized as an authentic human selfhood." The courage to be black, then, is the courage to affirm one's black being in the face of all that would seek to deny that black being is also human. The most powerful self-affirmation is for a person to have the courage to assert a self that is human in spite of that which would declare it to be less because of some mere particular such as color. Frantz Fanon is right when he reminds us that "man is human only to the extent to which he tries to impose his existence on another in order to be recognized by him." [6]

Black Self-love

Radical black self-affirmation, as it is now being evidenced in the black community, creates several possible problems for the black man as he relates to his white brother in a pro-white culture. Vincent Harding, Director of the "Institute of the Black World," puts the problem in focus when he

[4] *Ibid.,* p. 15.
[5] Paul Tillich, *The Courage to Be* (New Haven: Yale University Press, 1952), p. 3.
[6] Fanon, *Black Face, White Mask,* pp. 216 ff.

points out that "at the heart of the matter under discussion is the issue of how we can prepare black people to live with integrity on the scene of our former enslavement and our present estrangement." [7] Maybe a deeper question lies at the point of the development of the right black frame of reference out of which might possibly come an authentic self-affirmation, an affirmation that in its positive essence might counter any negative response.

Another of the live issues in the black community is a possible programmatic start. There is broad agreement that the black man needs to come to terms with himself. In the black community one cannot miss the fact that the ferment is a calling for black self-love. But it is far from an unambiguous summons; it needs broad clarification even for black people. Perhaps it is only a kind of focus on self first, because many black people would agree with the Black Power exponent who complained that "Martin King was trying to get us to love white folks before we learned to love ourselves, and that ain't no good." Dr. Harding rightfully observes that "in spite of some public images to the contrary, it is likely that no element is so constant in the gospel of Blackness—at least as it is encounered in its native communities—as the necessity of self-love." [8] Another writer puts it differently when she points to "the inner power that comes with self-esteem, the power to develop to full stature as human beings." [9]

Another facet of the question of authentic black personhood as it relates to the matter of self-love and self-esteem and ultimate self-acceptance is the further contention in the

[7] "The Religion of Black Power," in *The Religious Situation 1968*, ed. Donald R. Cutler (Boston: Beacon Press, 1968), p. 20.

[8] *Ibid.*, p. 4.

[9] Anita Cornwell, "Symposium on Black Power," *Negro Digest*, Nov., 1966.

black community that, because the black man has been so
demeaned by the indignities often directed at him because of
his color, he needs first to come to terms with himself as a
black man. He must love himself in the full sense of his
blackness. He must, if need be, hate anything and anybody
that cannot accept him as he is in his full blackness of person. For him to achieve this attitude, he must turn away from
his white brother and, if need be, hate him while learning to
love himself. After all, is it not natural for a man to hate
that which diminishes him? This is pointed out by many
who have contended that even the white man's love is to be
rejected because it too is demeaning. A song from the black
community puts it:

> Too much love,
> Too much love,
> Nothing kills a nigger like
> Too much love.

However, when asked, most who adhere to the struggle
would conclude with John Oliver Killens, one of the major
literary spokesmen for the movement, that black power "does
not teach hatred; it teaches love. But it teaches us that love,
like charity, must begin at home; that it must begin with
ourselves, our beautiful black selves." [10]

It is interesting to note also that the love that is advanced
by the black awareness movement requires nothing short of
love in return for love given. In the same essay Killens goes
on to say that the love taught by black power is "so powerful
that it will settle for nothing short of love in return. Therefore, it does not advocate unrequited love, which is a sick bit

[10] Killens, in "Symposium on Black Power."

under any guise or set of circumstances. Most black folk have no need to love those who would spit on them or practice genocide against them. . . . Profound love can only exist between equals."

One wonders at this point whether it is at all possible to love self alone? Is self-love possible only in relation to the self that is loving? This question applies equally to a group. Jesus, you will recall, raised the question of self-love only in relation to neighbor. Is it possible for the Negro to love himself, even as a group, and close out his white brother without having something radically wrong happen to his self-loving process? Can human requirements be fully met by black people loving only black people? One is not sure that self-love can meet the ultimate test of achieving the high self-esteem that black awareness advocates. Nor is one sure of the larger claim that self-love is an adequate way.

Vincent Harding brings the problem into focus in quite another way when he poses the cogent questions:

How shall the black and white victims of American racism best find their healing before the last night settles in? What is the nature of the binding process and under what conditions shall it best take place? One wonders, for instance, if the restoration of broken, embittered spirits can take place apart from the presence—at some point—of the offending, denying, guilt-dominated brother. Or is it impossible for black men to build the necessary strength to love themselves—which must precede all else—except through studied alienation from their former oppressors, even the truly repentant ones? Perhaps an even more sobering and "practical" question is whether or not a white community without inner quietness will allow the black workers time and space to build a unique (and thereby threatening) set of structures and beings.[11]

[11] Harding, "The Religion of Black Power," pp. 19-20.

The Harding questions are difficult, and it is doubtful whether they will be heeded by many of those who contend that self-love and the glorification of blackness have validity in any context other than in that of complete separation. This group would further argue that a glorification of blackness can take place only within a restricted context. It is, as Dr. Harding rightly points out, a question of exactly what is involved in the relation of black power to black and broken men who have been made ashamed of their blackness. Is it indeed glorified? Nathan Wright, chairman of the Black Power Conference, gives a theological interpretation to this point in contending that "the glorification of blackness implicit in the term Black Power is a conscious or unconscious effort to stake a claim for the worth of those in our nation who are termed non-white. Essentially it is a clarification. The root meaning of the term 'glorify' is to clarify, to make clear and plain straight." [12]

Dr. Wright would have confined his implications to the merely human sphere had he stopped there, but he goes on to say: "All of life must be clarified in this sense. It must be given and seen in that dimension which sets it forth in terms of glory—now and forever. To see life as it truly is means to see it as God sees it, in its eternal dimension, in the glory appropriate to its involvement with and in the life of God." [13]

This sets blackness in a new and different light, the light of the Creator. In this sense black men are called upon to see themselves as they were meant to be. This glorification, as black awareness advocates would have it, has the potential of setting them at peace with themselves and with the creative

[12] *Black Power and Urban Unrest* (New York: Hawthorn Books, 1967), p. 139.
[13] *Ibid.*, pp. 139-40.

purpose of the universe; they no longer need to hate themselves or to curse God and die, for they should be at home with their blackness. Indeed, is not their very blackness, like the rest of their createdness, the sign of God's love and not of God's anger?

If taken seriously, then, black awareness should make the black man more fit for the whole human context rather than the smaller arena of the black community. It should make him more fit to compete than some black power advocates would suggest. Decisive separation should not be necessary, for there should be the potential within the movement itself to decry separation.

However, one must remember that black awareness is still a new concept within the black community, and it needs years before it becomes a reality in program or attitude. The question that yet remains is, What will this separation, if one concedes that it is necessary, do to the black man? Will it make him a stronger or a weaker person?

Self-defense and Healthy Black Self-esteem

Though violence will be discussed more fully in a later chapter, it is necessary to relate the growing conflict between those who still adhere to the way of nonviolence and those who advocate violence as it might relate to the concept of self-esteem, self-identity, and self-affirmation. Such a discussion belongs in this context, because in the black community the concept of violence is so closely identified with the self-defense and the development of the new concept of black personhood or being.

The first question that comes to mind is that of self-defense and its relation to being and the deeper dimensions of selfhood. There would be no theological implications in the concept if it had not been given spiritual dimensions by those who relate it to the quest for authentic black self-identity. Moving the idea directly into focus, Killens contends that "men are not free until they affirm the right to defend themselves." And at the much deeper level of a full understanding of the problems of self-defense in relation to the broader questions posed by the black awareness movement, Killens gives a much more profound psychological meaning to self-defense for black men when he states clearly that "we black folk have a deep need to defend ourselves. Indeed, we have an obligation. We must teach the brutalizers how it feels to be brutalized. We must teach them that it hurts. They'll never know unless we teach them." [14] These statements are given even deeper implications when Dr. Harding interestingly points out that

there is, however, an even more profound issue in what Killens describes so sensitively as "a deep need" for black men to defend themselves. What he seems to be implying is this: when men have long been forced to accept the wanton attacks of their oppressors, when they have had to stand by and watch their women prostituted, it is crucial to their own sense of self-esteem that they affirm and be able to implement their affirmation of a right to strike back.

The basic human search for a definition of manhood is here set out in significant black lineaments. Does manhood indeed depend upon the capacity to defend one's life? Is this American shibboleth really the source of freedom for men? Is it possible that a man simply becomes a slave to another man's initiative when he feels obliged to answer his opponent on the opponent's terms? Is there perhaps a certain kind of bondage involved when men are so anxious about keeping themselves alive that they are ready to

[14] "Symposium on Black Power."

take the lives of others to prevent that occurrence? The question is really one of the image man was meant to reflect; what is it? [15]

Is self-defense the only way to true manhood? This is a question as deep as the nature of man himself. To be sure, it must not center in a mere response in kind. The truly strong man does not have to fear, for he seeks a higher manhood, a manhood that is given example in the life of the God-man Jesus Christ, who introduced even the Zealots of his time to a new and higher response. Black Power seems unwilling even to consider his way. Indeed, can only the strong, whole man afford not to strike back—the man who has not suffered oppression, who has no need for wholeness? What of the weak person who has a need for wholeness?

The question of self-defense, as it is being debated in the black community today, is a sharp question for many reasons. First of all, it not only relates to being itself, but it also has to do with the problem of the liberation of a people. So the question of what the lack of self-defense does to a person's basic selfhood is a serious question for a black man seeking authentic self-identity. Second, the issue is not just what self-defense contributes to a person's own basic selfhood; it is also a question of how self-defense is related to freedom or liberation. In this sense, then, the nonviolence-violence debate is far from being over. We turn now to the nonviolence-violence issues.

Nonviolence and Self-defense

Indeed, does the nonviolent approach, as Martin Luther King put it, "do something to the hearts and souls of those

[15] Harding, "The Religion of Black Power," pp. 21-22.

who are committed to it?" Does it "give them 'self-respect,'"
will it "call up resources of strength and courage that they
did not know they had"? [16]

Very few people will accept fully Dr. King's contention
that nonviolence is not a capitulation to weakness and fear,
that it demands of its advocates that difficult kind of stead-
fastness which can endure indignation with dignity. Fewer
still, especially now, would accept Dr. King's contention that
the "endurance of unearned suffering is redemptive." Neither
would many others follow his contention that not only does
nonviolence avoid the demeaning results that one suffers
when he lends himself to external physical violence, but nonviolence also helps one avoid internal violence of the spirit.

It would seem that most of the current critics of Dr. King
and his nonviolent views are persons who looked upon his
nonviolent way as being a mere method for social action,
and thus not a way of life, as it became for Dr. King. This is
why there is such a broad misreading of the literature of
nonviolence, and why so many people consider it less than
applicable to many of the current problems of the black
man's plight. It is quite true that to embrace nonviolence as
a mere methodology may not contribute to the positive thrust
of self-affirmation. However, to accept it as a way of life, a
moral-theological principle, is another matter. It is here that
the non-theologians have misread Dr. King's thought; for indeed, the ultimate aim of nonviolence is not conquest, it is
rather to establish a relationship. And, related to Christian
love, nonviolence may well be required to avoid a motive of
conquest or defeat and the need for defense of self.

[16] See Dr. King's "Pilgrimage to Nonviolence," *Christian Century*,
April 13, 1960, p. 439.

Violence and Self-defense

When the leaders of what Dr. Harding calls the "Religion of Black Power" speak of self-defense, it would seem they speak of it individually and collectively. The emphasis in this discussion will relate to the individual, for it is here that the basic self-image is developed. It is here that they are at cogent odds with the King position on the individual internalized personal strength and the integrity of personhood to be derived from adopting nonviolence as a way of life. Their basic position can be summarized at two levels. First, externally speaking, many adherents of the black awareness movement would contend that a person must be free to defend his person against all external threats. They contend that no healthy self-esteem can be developed without this basic freedom. Not to be free to defend oneself is to be saddled with a paralyzing fear, which demeans the basic stuff of personhood. This is what they would contend that Paul Tillich means by "the ethical act of self-affirmation," and what they would understand Frantz Fanon to mean by "imposing one's existence on another." The freedom to be violent is essential to a healthy self-esteem, many black people would contend today. Second, internally speaking, many adherents of the black awareness movement would assert that the freedom to choose hate or love is essential; the value of each would depend upon the response needed or called for within the context of the moment. And here, one can see, the expression is from a nontheological frame of reference, for the Christian's contention that hate is demeaning is totally unacceptable. For black awareness adherents, to hate the enemy is a human reaction and is thus normal. To defend oneself against the destructive actions of the enemy is normal; any other action is abnormal and produces a weak, reduced self-affirmation. To accept the abuses of the white man; to accept his attempt not to recognize the black man's personhood; to accept his violence, external or internal, without a response in kind, black awareness adherents contend, is to do the basic stuff of personhood a disservice and is thus demeaning. Indeed, is Dr. Harding right when he points out, in his assessment of the mind-set of the ghetto, that "as we have seen, black men have been chained to weakness for so long that any talk of voluntarily choosing a way that the society counts as weak is considered sheer madness"? [17]

It may well be true, as some blacks would hold, that the nonviolent approach, the lack of self-defense, is indeed demeaning. But from an assessment of the question, it would seem that modification would have to be conceded, and such an assertion would only apply to the weak, or indeed to the person who would remain weak. It takes more strength to remain nonviolent in response to external violence from the enemy than it does to respond in kind; for, as Dr. Harding has pointed out above, to respond in kind may well make the oppressor the master.[18] Does he not determine what kind the response should be? Thus, to feel the need to respond to violence by becoming violent seems to make one a slave to the person or persons who called forth the act of violence as a means of self-defense. The self-defense adherents cannot escape the cogent question as to just who is the master.

Jesus was a good example; at no place did he allow the external to determine what he should say or how he should act at a given moment. Is this not what moved him to pray from the cross, "Forgive them?" Was this not the reason he

[17] Harding, "The Religion of Black Power," p. 27.
[18] *Ibid.*, p. 22.

admonished Peter to "put up thy sword: for all they that take the sword shall perish with the sword"? Few would suggest that this prayer or this advice to Peter came from a weak frame of reference.

The True Meaning of Freedom

Freedom must not again be an illusion for the black man; it must be a reality. And it must be not only an empty, formal freedom from something. It must be, if it is a meaningful reality, a rich and definite freedom for something. We must examine what such an assertion means in the light of the current black awareness movement. (a) Who is free? This question is, and always has been, upon the lips of many who have sought only an illusion of the reality. Is not a man free who has achieved independence from any kind of external tyranny, so that he thinks and acts accordingly? (b) Or rather is a man not free if, as a thinking man—quite apart from whether or not he is free politically or socially—he has been liberated himself from the tyranny of passions and emotions? (c) Or rather is a man not most free when he is independent of the evil world and the demonic powers that control his fate? When he alone can set his own directions?

Man is far from being free simply because he has thrown off threats and pressures outside himself. The real threats to freedom are those which come from within man himself, and this is one of the reasons why a clear conception of freedom is so vital to the black man's quest for true self-identity. The black man has now at last proved himself equal to many of the external tyrannies that have for years confused his mind and inner spirit. There are many reasons for this achievement. First of all, as has been stated before, the ethical climate in America has matured enough to permit the black man to be honest, so that for the first time in his whole life in America he can tell the world how he had felt as a victim of the black experience. His ready access to the press and other means of communication have helped him to make the black experience articulate; and to articulate the black experience has been therapeutic for the black man's mind-set. Second, the black man has now become a serious seeker for a more authentic selfhood; thus, the inner "two-persons" confusion, of which Dr. DuBois spoke in his book *The Souls of Black Folk,* is no longer a problem. The black man, with few exceptions, knows now that he does not or that he ought not to seek to be white, like his oppressor; he rather should seek a true blackness. Third, if the freedom now sought by so many black people is fully realized, there will never be a time when the black man will accept the oppressor in quite the same way as he has accepted him in prior years. There may well be subsequent oppression and tyranny, but it will be rejected in quite a different way and with more force than ever before. This is what the heart of the current struggle is all about. If it is fully embraced, and if it is fully internalized, black awareness does become an ideology akin to an obsession, or indeed a religion. This is why Dr. Harding talks, and rightly so, of "the religion of Black Power"; it has become a kind of substitute for traditional religion. Though many black people would have deep questions before accepting such a label, most would agree that there is a new hope dawning in the black community. However, it is an uneasy, unrealized hope because of the many persisting and potential external conditions that could serve to frustrate much of the hope and aspirations of black people in our current pro-white culture. It is an uneasy hope because of its new dawning; it is an uneasy hope because it has never been fully tried before.

Indeed, the black man has just now acquired the audacity to hope in the climate of an uncertain, newly acquired freedom.

The Ultimate Goal of Black Self-assertion

At the beginning of this chapter, the question was raised, What type of ultimate personhood does the black man seek? This is a hard question to answer, for the simple reason that no final characteristics of the new black personhood have yet revealed themselves. However, C. R. H. Long of the University of Chicago comes nearest to grasping the problem when he makes the rather interesting assertion that the plight of the black man, in his current search for self-identity, is inherent in the fact that he is neither fully African nor a true American. Culturally he has been cut off from Africa, and yet not completely. He tends yet to identify with African people, but it is with a sense kinship that is void of full ethnic or cultural authenticity. Dr. Long puts Africa in the American black man's future rather than in his past.

Dr. Long further illustrates this by pointing out that when one goes to Africa, he senses that he has been cut off from his African heritage because he is not able to communicate with a people who are so much like himself; he is aware that he has lost the art or the ability to communicate with them by articulation, by emotion, or by extrasensory perception. The fuller identification is to be found in the future in still closer contacts.

By the same token, Dr. Long argues that the black man is not totally a product of American culture, because of his alien kinship with the past, which has been blurred by the dehumanizing process of the black experience. America has never fully accepted him; he is and always has been the "other American."

In the current black awareness movement it is the ultimate aim of the black man to free himself of this ambiguity of being by finding a selfhood that can really be neither American nor African. It just may be that the Afro-American concept connotes the meaning of the "high synthesis of black Afro-American Personhood"—as Professor Hazaiah Williams of the Berkeley Theological Union would put it—which is beyond the current struggle. What stronger hope could there be for the black community?

This new black manhood, which represents something infinitely new and different in the modern world, totally unlike what can be seen in the current examples of those who seek a black identity, could well be the ultimate end of the black man's present seeking. It does not yet appear what it shall be. This is the hope of the future. It is a hope that is becoming real at so many levels of the black community that one cannot help being fully aware of the fact that something radical and new is taking place among black people. It is indeed a "religion of blackness" under God which is pushing its way into every possible facet of black endeavor; it has become a byword for many levels of encounter. It is becoming a reality, though many blacks are rejecting it.

7

THE IMPLICATIONS OF A THEOLOGY OF HOPE FOR THE BLACK COMMUNITY

The Fused Concepts of Hope and Revolution

The current development in the movement toward black awareness has been characterized by a kind of learned hope that presses its adherents, as Christians, to acknowledge the ontological priority of a kind of future mode of black being which has not yet revealed itself in the fullness of maturity. This fact has already been indicated above. However, it should be made clearer that this hope is currently at the very heart of the mood of black existence.

This is made more true because this hope is akin to the black revolution, whether violent or nonviolent, and it also seeks to make itself known to the nonblack world. Further, hope and revolution are sometimes fused concepts for black people for the simple reason that so many black people do not feel that the two concepts can be separated in a complex, inflexible, fixed, and unchangeable social structure such as ours. Meaningful change is so hard to come by that many have about lost faith in a hope unrelated to violence, revolution, or extreme social pressure.

It is time for the Christian man, black or white, to take note when fellow Christians seek to find an adequate theological justification for a hope that also embraces some concept of a violent revolution. Hope in too much of the black community is a violent hope, and yet it is a hope that seeks an outlet at every level of human life. It is a total hope that is founded on the arrival of the absolute and finalized future of the black man within history. Whether such a hope can be Christian will depend in part upon what the Christian churches, black and white, are willing to contribute to its ultimate fulfillment within the context of this world. If it is centered in the church or theological concepts of our time, such a hope might well be labeled "black eschatology." And yet, in this context, it must be conceived as an eschatological message that is utterly and completely human. It leads us, not away from man, but toward the perfect image of man symbolized in the person of the Jesus of history. It does not direct attention away from the earth, because it conceives that somehow the greatest wisdom is bound up with a cross staked in the ground and a grave dug into the earth.

There are many things that can be said of this newly learned hope, which if understood, will make one understand why many knowledgeable blacks view it with such interest and with such optimism. And surely if one understood this hope he would not dare dismiss it as a mere passing fad. This is not to say that it has yet come into full view as any kind of mature expression; it is rather to say that it has revealed itself enough to let one get a glimpse of its ultimate potential for a people who yesterday had no hope.

Above all, it must be said that a black theology of hope, based on the black awareness movement, is not theological in a Moltmann or a Bloch sense of a theology of hope. This is so because the traditional language of theology is not very intelligible to the man in the street, and especially to the current black man of hope. An intelligible black theology of hope has been almost nonexistent, and yet for some time now black Christians have needed to take a look at the problems that might confront any attempts to develop an adequate theology of hope. This is not surprising when we recall that for too long white theologians have been producing systems in which the alien virtues of harmony, order, and stability have been stressed.

It may well be that black people have come to a time when, if the black theologian is to speak to their current conditions, he must at least develop a theology of hope that will embrace in some sense the concept of revolution in its fullest implications. Harvey Cox has seen this problem, which is faced not only by the black Christian in America, but by all Christians. He contends that "we are trying to live in a period of revolution without a theology of revolution. The development of such a theology should be the first item on the theological agenda today." [1] But the average Christian, black or white, might well venture the question of just why do we need a theology of revolution. For many minds such a thought is a terrifying mixture of categories or a confusion of horizons. Indeed, they ask, how can we define a theology of revolution as a theology related to an earthly eschatological hope within the context of our present society?

Within the black community, especially outside the church, there is too little time for the reflective type of theologizing of the past. We have come to a point where there is a tendency to fuse the concepts of hope and revolution. For the average black man in the ghetto, for any theology to be

[1] Harvey Cox, *The Secular City* (New York: Macmillan, 1965), p. 107.

meaningful it must speak to only those factors or actions which are going to help him realize a better day within his lifetime; he would insist that the only time he has is now. In this light, then, there is a very practical reason for the urgent need for a theology of hope that is closely related to revolution. Without such hope, it would seem, the black churchman will be at a total loss about what to do with the concept of revolution for a long time to come. It may be that this is the reason there is such a cry against the black church, the black college, and many other black institutions—they simply have not found adequate words to articulate what they think of the future. It may well be because, as has been said, they have not seen hope as a viable possibility without revolutionary actions that are totally alien to their present mode of thought. Indeed, did the black theologians really mean it when they asserted with Eldridge Cleaver: "We shall have our manhood. We shall have it or the earth will be leveled by our efforts to gain it"? [2] One is moved to ask of them whether they are at one with Hannah Arendt in her book *On Revolution,* when she predicts that even though mankind has the good sense to set aside war as an international political instrument, revolutions will continue into the foreseeable future to make this a century of revolution. Then she says that "in the contests which divide the world today, and in which so much is at stake, those will probably win who understand revolution." [3] Black Christians must at least understand revolution, not with the intent to win a political revolution as such, but rather because, if it takes place, they cannot escape accepting or acquiring some responsibility for its outcome.

[2] Produced by the Committee of Theological Prospectus, June 13, 1969, at the Interdenominational Theological Center, Atlanta, Georgia.

[3] Hannah Arendt, *On Revolution* (New York: Viking Press, 1963), p. 8.

The stakes are always high in revolutionary times—the future of mankind, the scale of justice, the quality of freedom; and ultimately there is at stake the shape of society beyond revolution. Indeed, the ultimate concern of the Christian, black or white, does not lie outside these secular interests; it rather relates to the problem of finding a formative expression through them. No matter what the context, the religious relationship between man and God does run alongside the relationship of both to the world. The commandment to love God has no substance at all apart from love of neighbor. Love of neighbor is always at stake in a revolution.

Though the church is to a large degree responsible for the revolutionary consciousness that is emerging around the world today, the people who seem now to be talking revolution, especially in the black community, are largely nontheological in their views. Thus, their view of revolution has very little of the content of a theology of hope. And yet in many ways, whether violent or nonviolent, a theology of hope must be related to a theology of revolution.

In the chapter "The Revolutionary West," in his book *Christianity in World History*, A. T. Van Leeuwen ascribes the revolutionary impulse in the West to the revolutionizing impact of the gospel of the coming kingdom of God.[4] Indirectly the church has sponsored the revolutionary process by preaching a message that sets things in motion by stirring up the imagination, arousing new expectations, and stimulating a crusading zeal to translate hopes—whose realization some would postpone for heaven above—into the social structures of this world. The simple fact of preaching the gospel is itself like putting sticks of explosives into the social structure. The

[4] Arend Th. Van Leeuwen, *Christianity in World History*, trans. by H. H. Hoskins (New York: Scribner's, 1966), p. 344.

church is indeed responsible for having planted the seed within the beloved structures that it, at the same time, had no desire to explode, since its own privileges were beholden to them. The church has too long preached a gospel of revolution without meaning to do so, and, more than that, without knowing clearly what it was talking about when it mentioned some of the revolutionary themes of the Bible and the Christian faith.

A theology of revolution is made all the more urgent by the additional fact that the Christian churches must repent of the inglorious role they have played in most modern revolutionary situations. While the gospel they preached pointed the way to hope for the future, the institutions they built impeded its coming. The white church and the black church have, at times, been at one in proclaiming a revolutionary gospel of equality. Neither one, however, has fully adhered to the reality in the area of race relations. If they had, both now would be more deeply engaged in the black liberation struggles of our time. Hope and revolution must be brought into some kind of understandable relationship.

When we speak specifically of the black church and a theology of hope, we must take a hard look at what revolution means for the black community, for this is where the issue is in such sharp current focus.

First of all, it must be understood that there is a sharp distinction between rebellion and revolution. The aim of a rebellion is to restore what has been lost; the aim of revolution is to create something new. The vision of the radically new, inherent in revolution, is what links revolutionary action to eschatological hope. Revolution is a relevant concept within the context of the black community.

Second, when revolution is mentioned in the black community, it is not confined, and many times not even related, to current theological expressions of hope; it is rather an expression related only to despair and hopelessness. This is why revolution should now be related to a theology of hope, lest we end up with despair and hopelessness.

Indeed, the reason revolution is such an issue in the black community is that most black people have given up hope in the ability of any protest movement void of violent revolution. This feeling of utter despair was cogently caught up in the Preamble of the "Black Manifesto," presented to the white churches of America a few years ago. A part of their reason for rejecting many of the demands of the "Black Manifesto" was that the Preamble called for revolution. It insisted "that revolution is the only remedy for our social ills." [5] In its response to the reparation demands, Riverside Church of New York City was right in pointing out that "we believe that when desperate people talk this way, intransigence and rigidity on the part of the establishment only tend to prove the revolutionary's point—that the situation is hopeless." [6]

The Black Christian's Dilemma with Revolution

The newer theologians who are impressed with the language of hope speak of God as "the absolute future," and at times one is led to feel that there is nothing man can do, that the pressure of the future brings creation out of nothing, making for a kind of inexhaustible source of innovation in the world. But when we talk of revolution within the context of the present world, Christians are confronted with several

[5] See the Preamble to the "Black Manifesto" by James Forman, et al.

[6] From the Riverside Church's response to James Forman's May 4, 1969, reparations demands at Riverside Church.

options. First, a Christian can be relevant to the revolution as a mere cheerleader for it. Second, the Christian can become engaged to a limited degree, setting limits beyond which he will not go. Third, no matter how a Christian may relate to a revolution, he must recognize that revolution in the modern world may mean possible violence, and violence means killing. However, if there were no danger of killing, one could never exclude the possibility that after the revolution, the newly structured society might become a new status quo, as in the case of Cuba. Often the Christian has no choice; he must either take sides and fight for an evil and oppressive regime, or take sides with what he feels to be a potentially better political or social order. Indeed, when a Christian wants to enter the political arena at all, he must cope with the possibility of a breakdown of peace or of politics and the ultimate possibility that violence, which means killing, will ensue—and he will be a part. It would seem that there can be no theology of revolution unless it comes to grips with the question of whether it is at all possible to extend a theological or an ethical justification for killing.

The Conflicting Ideologies of Violence and Nonviolence

The black or white Christian theologians who attempt to construct a theology of revolution must face the ultimate risk of whether violence can produce enough good to justify the means. Without exception, any theology of revolution has to face the question whether under any condition, circumstances, or occasion it could ever support theologically or ethically the act of killing a neighbor. For when one enters the political arena, especially the revolutionary political arena, in any way at all, he must cope with the possibility that violence will ensue. Whether the call for revolution be a first or a last resort, the question the black Christian faces, in relation to violence, is whether he can, as a Christian, kill another person. Does killing ever become right in any war, even a "just" war? Whether the killing is intentional or unintentional, the problem is the same for the Christian. Even in contextual or situational ethics, if one is committed to act under the mandate of love for neighbor, the necessity of killing another person is problematic for the Christian. If one is committed to the love of neighbor, then it would seem impossible to reconcile the act of killing the neighbor that one is committed to love. Indeed, is it ever possible to kill a person one is committed by God to love? Is it at all possible for one to give adherence to the concept of the sacredness of persons, and at the same time will the destruction of a person? It would seem that it is impossible for the Christian to answer such questions in the affirmative.

Within this context there has been no attempt to deal with conditions that may, under certain circumstances, make killing necessary. Granted that some wars or revolutions may be just and even necessary. When such action becomes necessary, and the Christian feels that he must not or cannot remain neutral, he must at that point adopt what Paul Ricoeur has called the "ethics of distress," [7] admitting to himself and to God that his actions beyond this point are not Christian. Such a stance would, it seems, prevent all impossible attempts to construct blanket theological justifications

[7] See Ricoeur's *History and Truth* (Evanston: Northwestern University Press, 1965), p. 243. Martin E. Marty concurs with this view in *The Search for a Usable Future* (New York: Harper, 1969), p. 115.

95

for so much that is wrong with war in general and killing in particular. Violence is necessarily contrary to love.

Indeed, to a black theologian, what is troubling is not that the opinions of Christians, black or white, are changing, or that their opinions are shaped by the current problems of a time—on the contrary, this is as it should be. What is more troubling is that too many Christians conform to the trend of the moment without introducing into it anything specifically Christian. Their ethical convictions are too often determined by their social milieu, not by faith in Christian revelation; they too often lack the uniqueness that ought to be more expressive of their religious faith. Thus, theologies, especially the newer expressions, tend too often to become mere mechanical exercises that justify the positions adopted on grounds that are absolutely not Christian. Much of what is now called theological justification for revolution would bespeak such a trend. Currently black churchmen and black theologians increasingly are finding it hard to resist offering theological justification for views akin to the black racism current within much of the black community. This is not to say that some counter-racism is probably not needed in the black community; it is rather to contend that black theology should not extend justification for it. Yet it is strange how far theologians will go in their attempt to be all things to all kinds of people.

The Humane Principle of Revolution

One finds it hard to disagree that

the humane principle of revolution is this way: the slave revolts against his master. He denies him as a master, but not as a man. For his protest is directed against the master's refusal to treat him as a man. As master and slave, neither is a true man and neither can relate to the other in a humane way. If the denial of the master were total, the slave's revolt would bring nothing new into the world but with exchange the roles of inhumanity. The humane revolution, however, is not out to turn slaves into masters but to abolish the whole master-slave relationship so that in the future men will be able to treat one another as men. If the revolution loses sight of this goal, it becomes nihilistic and forfeits its fascination.[8]

In addition to this interesting exposition of Albert Camus's concept of a humane principle of revolution, Moltmann further contends that under certain conditions the use of revolutionary violence can be justified by humane goals. However, he is not too sure that such justification can be assured, and so he concludes that unless it is possible and assured, "revolutionary violence cannot be made meaningful or appropriate. Unless every possible means is put to use, the revolutionary future is not worth committing oneself to." [9] However, one wonders if black theology can embrace Moltmann's position when he advises that "people must be able to combine what they desire with what is objectively possible and what they can subjectively accomplish." [10]

Indeed, if a revolution can be this rational and if the aims can be preconceived, then one wonders if some more rational approach cannot be found than a violent revolution. It would seem that Moltmann is nearer right when he reminds us that

if the revolutionary goal is a more fully realized humanity, then revolutionaries cannot afford to be inhuman during the so-called

[8] Jürgen Moltmann, *Religion, Revolution and the Future*, p. 142.
[9] *Ibid.*, p. 143.
[10] *Ibid.*, p. 144.

transitional period. Already, on the way, we must directly begin with the future and make life truly human during the transitional period. . . .

It follows, therefore, that a revolution of the present for the benefit of a better and more humane future must not mold itself after the strategies of the world to be overthrown. Only with great restraint can revolutionaries enter the diabolical circle of violence and counter-violence if they are ever to conquer and abolish it as a whole. . . . How are we to bring about the kingdom of non-violent brotherhood with the help of violent action? [11]

These words of Moltmann cannot be read without recalling the teachings of Martin Luther King, Jr., for it was he who, perhaps more than many people who talk of revolution today, thought and acted out of a deep dimension of truth which was not dependent on political power and the rules of its games. Too many people could not accept this fact—that his frame of reference was theological, and he was, to a great extent, immune from anxiety and the seduction of political power. Precisely for that reason alone he became more and more in disfavor, and a greater threat to people in positions of great power than even the prophets of violence themselves. In a very real sense, the true revolutionary must not allow the law of the opposition to prescribe his own course of action or response, otherwise he cannot become a part of the new humanity. Any means may be appropriate, but they must be different and better than those of the opposition if they would bewilder the opposition.

Toward an "Ethics of Distress"

It is not the thesis of this book to assess the need or the lack of a need for revolution, whether violent or nonviolent. There

[11] *Ibid.*

has been little attempt to discuss whether the present social or political systems of the world can or cannot be altered without violence. My main concern has been over the trend of modern theologians to attempt to extend theological or ethical justifications for violent revolution, thus further confusing persons into believing that they are being Christian when indeed they are not. Colin Morris, in his book *Unyoung, Uncolored, Unpoor*, has made a cogent plea for such an unconditional justification, so it might be helpful to assess his basic thesis within this context. He contends that "Christians have both the right and the responsibility to take part in revolution," be it violent or nonviolent in nature. He is right in his assertion that

we weep with pride in the story of Dietrich Bonhoeffer's triumphant death at the hands of the Flossenberg hangman, and pore over his last writings with an eagerness that could not be greater had he handed them out personally to us from the other side of the Beyond. But we scurry quickly away from the tougher truth that he was a justly condemned accessory to murder. Hitler, the main target of the plot, indeed survived Stauffenberg's bomb, but others in that map room were destroyed, some of them honorable soldiers. If only Bonhoeffer had lived, we lament, to tell us more about the line of thought sketched out in the startling epigrams of *Letters and Papers from Prison*. I, for one, believe that his explanation of the theology behind the bomb plot might have more to say to our time. The new theology for which the Church is searching may be hidden in that violent deed of Bonhoeffer's which misfired and not in his musings about God without religion. Any Christian, tasting the sulphur which hangs in the air of our time, could wish for a theology of violence from the pen of a great theologian who dared to strike and paid for his temerity with his life.[12]

[12] Colin Morris, *Unyoung, Uncolored, Unpoor* (Nashville: Abingdon Press, 1969), p. 24.

In his further contention, Dr. Morris talks about the timing of the Christian's action as being problematic because he has to delay long enough to make sure that the extent of the evil justifies the radical action. The problem is, how long should one delay doing what one feels that he has to do? Hitler should have been cut down sooner, and the six million Jews would have been spared, and the world would not have suffered so greatly at his hands. This is rightly a concern of the Christian. "Bonhoeffer, Stauffenberg, and the rest indeed died to rid the world of a fount of evil. Yet if they had struck ten years earlier, before the smoke and the gas chambers had blackened the sky and Europe's cities were aflame, who knows how history might have been changed?" [13]

One might well accept the actions of Bonhoeffer, one might have agreed with those who plotted Hitler's death, one might also have accepted the fact that Hitler was indeed a "fount of evil"; but to say that even such a great theologian as Bonhoeffer was acting like a Christian is a much deeper question and a much more serious problem. Indeed, it would seem that maybe had he lived he would have admitted that when the group gathered to plot Hitler's death they were not attempting to find theological justification for their actions, because there could be none. But they were honest Christians fully realizing that they were acting without any theological or ethical justification; and had they survived they would have been in need of deep forgiveness for actions that they might well have admitted were not Christian. But nevertheless, theirs were actions which they thought needed to be taken. Are there not times when Christian man

[13] *Ibid.*, p. 25.

has not to decide simply between right and wrong and between good and evil, but between right and right and between wrong and wrong. . . . Precisely in this respect responsible action is a free venture; it is not justified by any law; it is performed without any claim to a valid self-justification, and therefore also without any claim to an ultimate valid knowledge of good and evil. Good, as what is responsible, is performed in ignorance of good and in the surrender to God of the deed which has become necessary and which is nevertheless, or for that very reason, free.[14]

It matters not how frustrating the situation may become, it would seem that any lasting solution must be found, especially for the black man, in some approach other than violence, for violence is the very language of the enemy, and against violence he seems to have an adequate response that would assure all rational thinkers that liberation cannot come by the way of violence.

This is not to withdraw from those actions which are necessary to counter the evils of racism, and this is not to rule out the fact that some of these actions may even be violent. It is just to argue that any actions against the enemy should further the cause of freedom, rather than restrict it.

So the concern here is not with a lack of action, it is rather that actions be seen rationally and honestly for what they are and not justified for what they are not. Thus, an "ethics of distress" is more honest to both self and God. And the lack of success, while engaging in actions that are ill advised, will not commit God to failures for which he may or may not be totally responsible.

Paul Ricoeur, in his book *History and Truth*, has described the violent moment as a time when an ethics of distress is

[14] Dietrich Bonhoeffer, *Ethics*, ed. by Eberhard Bethge and trans. by N. H. Smith (New York: Macmillan, 1955), p. 249.

invoked, and such an ethics would suggest that conditions are such that remedies cannot be justified theologically. His contention is that such honesty is better than an ethics or a theology which anticipates the legitimacy either of killing or of a pure passivism and the victim role. There are times, one must agree, when conventional ethical norms cannot be applied, especially in the black community. Indeed, there are situations in which one must do what one must do and then say one's prayers.

The current problem facing the black community is one of change, which will make like bearable for many black people in white America. For the oppressed and for those who appear now to have no hope, there seems to be no way except to embrace violence as a means of social change. To tell them it is futile and that it will bring no real change is an impossible position. They have tried other ways.

They saw the way of nonviolence suffer a bitter blow in the death of Dr. King. They also recall that Stokely Carmichael and H. Rap Brown both were once adherents to the nonviolent way of protest. In later years, they contended on many occasions that nonviolent protest was always met with violence from the white community, which resisted any change whatsoever. Intellectual guerrilla warfare, properly located spokesmen for change, the government, the police forces, all have failed in their support of any great and meaningful change for the vast majority of the black community.

The one question that faces the black community is still whether there are yet more effective nonviolent means for perfecting social change. There are many who still think that all the means have not been exhausted. Vincent Harding contends that massive nonviolent means have not been fully tried, and his is still a strong voice for further exploration of nonviolent means of protest for social change. But there are others, for instance the Black Panthers, who have come to feel that there is no hope short of violent revolution for changing current social structures; it is for them that hope is needed. But, while black Christian radicalism, even if it takes love seriously, forbids participation in violence of any kind, it cannot ever give counsel to the oppressed to be submissive and accepting. Too often in history Christians have betrayed their faith by preaching resignation to the oppressed without giving due attention to the oppressor.

Nonviolence as a Revolutionary Method

Adherents of the way of nonviolence, whether it be conceived as a methodology or as a way of life, root their actions in a strong Christian belief that one should absorb hatred and transform it through love, that one should endure rather than inflict violence. This basic faith in the nonviolent way leads to two approaches. First, centering on persons, the proponents of nonviolence contend that nonviolence cannot be an external attitude; it must be internalized. It is in being himself at peace that a person becomes peaceful; it is in living by the law and mandate of love that a person becomes capable of manifesting that love; it is through the practice of it in one's personal life that nonviolence spreads to others. Second, it must be recalled that the whole problem of nonviolence comes down to two conclusions: (a) the state must be divested of its instruments of violence, and (b) for their part, proponents of nonviolence must respond to other people's use of violence by nonviolent actions—sacrifice, noncooperation, civil disobedience, etc. Nonviolence has not been tried on a wide scale since Gandhi. No hope for the future, whether with or without violence, can adequately speak to the black community unless it takes seriously the oppressed people's contentions against the oppressors.

On the assumption that the Christian cannot choose the way of violence, the ethics of revolutionary involvement is particularly problematic for those who advocate a nonviolent approach. Especially is it so if they do not believe that military action solves as much as it purports to achieve, and if they further contend that a man does not have a right to arrogate to himself the decision concerning who should live and who should die. The Christian who gives adherence to violence always must run the risk that violence will demand the end to the potentiality of another person, a person who may himself have been able to contribute to the world's good. The black Christian cannot propose to live by any other standard than those ethical principles, or the unconditional mandate of love, if he lives by any principle at all. It would seem that no ethical frame of reference which makes the development rather than the destruction of the person one of its central concerns can adhere to any concept of violent revolution. When the black Christian thinks otherwise, then he must embrace an ethics of distress, admitting that he has passed beyond Christian action. However, for nonviolence, as a method or as a way of life, to work, it would have to be adopted with the belief that: (1) a government can maintain itself without ever using violence against its citizens; (2) there is such a thing as a "just state" that would be sufficient unto itself; (3) the structures of society are still flexible enough for there to be a deep moral ethos that makes society receptive.

Few people of the black community would now accept such a basic presupposition. Most black people with whom one talks are more ready to believe that most levels of white society are ready for what Lerone Bennett calls "confrontation" [15] between the races, and that the majority of the black people know this will mean violence against the black community. Thus, there seems to be little hope for the black man ever retrogressing to the way of nonviolence as a means of protest or revolution.

There is no suggestion in this context that violence should be the methodology now adopted; it is rather to suggest that the "black mood" has created a new man who is through with humiliation, and he is seeking rescue through whatever means necessary, even revolution. This type of revolution is not, and cannot be, a strategy consciously devised. It will grow out of the deep, instinctive expression of human being denied individuality. Such expressions of revolution, violent or nonviolent, can be liberating. Or as Lerone Bennett puts it: "The boundary of freedom is man's power to say 'No!' and whoever refuses to say 'No' involves himself tragically in his own degradation." [16] From all levels of the black community there will increasingly come the answer "No!" to any type of degrading actions on the part of the white community.

The basic thesis of this book is that such a "No!" does not have to be violent if it is a collective "No!" and if it comes from the lips of a liberated people who really mean "No!" Such an ethos is collecting within the black community; it

[15] Lerone Bennett, *Confrontation: Black and White* (Baltimore: Penguin Books, 1966). See also Bennett's *Negro Mood*, p. 95.
[16] *Ibid.*, p. 256.

is the "now" and the "not-yet" facet of the hope that is inherent in the black awareness movement.

The hope within the black awareness movement is theological, because it is, as one can conceive it, under God. The final pages of this book will be devoted to an exposition of the implications of such a hope for the black Christian.

8

THE FUTURE OF THE CONCEPT OF GOD IN THE BLACK COMMUNITY

Black Liberation, the Concept of God, and the Idea of a People Chosen

Basic to the black man's struggle to liberate himself from his oppressor is the age-old idea of God's chosen people. From Old Testament times until our time, the idea has occurred among many peoples, both privileged and oppressed, in quite different ways and for many different reasons. Black awareness has picked up this kind of hope, and it is left for the current black theologians to interpret such a hope from a black theological frame of reference. As Dr. King so often put it:

This is the challenge. If we will dare to meet it honestly, historians in future years will have to say that there lived a great people—a black people—who bore their burdens of oppression in the heat of many days and who, through tenacity and creative commitment, injected new meaning into the veins of American life.[1]

[1] Martin Luther King, *Where Do We Go from Here: Chaos or Community* (New York: Harper, 1967), p. 134.

However, long before and since Dr. King penned the lines above, with a quite different admonition to the oppressed, we have had other kinds of calls to a different kind of revolution. There have been calls to black people from many types of black leaders, and such calls have been to many kinds of action, but all such calls are from leaders of a black people who rightly or wrongly have thought of themselves as having been chosen by God to lead a chosen black people. Thus, one cannot study the history of the black man's protest, especially in America, without reading of the many black messiahs who have come forth to offer deliverance to the black man from the bondage of his white oppressor. Our current time, though few would admit it, is not without its many voices claiming a kind of liberation or freedom from oppression. Some have related the liberation of the black man to a kind of reciprocal or simultaneous liberation for the white oppressor. But this has not always been the case. From the days of Marcus Garvey of the twenties to Ronald Fair of our own time, there have been those who thought of black liberation as being only unilateral and sometimes radical in nature. Writing in the *Negro Digest* about the meaning of black power, Fair expressed the ultimate hope in this light:

> We are the ones who will right all the wrongs perpetrated against us and our ancestors and we are the ones who will save the world and bring a new day, a brilliantly alive society that swings and sings and rings out the world over for decency and honesty and sincerity and understanding and beauty and love.[2]

Here you have a new age promised of God to a people chosen, and the liberation is for black people only. The love which binds the black people together is also a love for black

[2] "Symposium on Black Power," p. 94.

only. Fair says, "We fight on and we spread the love we have been told we cannot feel for ourselves to each and every black man we meet."

According to Fair, the fullness of time has come for the black community. He contends that "every black man in this country is aware that our time has come." There is a faith that reaches beyond America, and the black messianic hope becomes worldwide in its concern for black people everywhere. Killens expresses this when he writes:

We black Americans are no longer a "minority" but a part of that vast majority of humanity yearning to be free and struggling with every ounce of their strength to throw off the black man's burden and the yoke of white supremacy. We are a part of that fellowship of the disinherited which will surely inherit the earth in this century.[3]

It is interesting to note that most black awareness advocates have little concern for the liberation of whites, whatever this might mean in relation to freedom for the black man. Black awareness advocates are concerned only for what is to take place in the black community. Some express this lack of concern in hate, or in the loss of hope for obtaining any real help from the white community in the black man's fight for freedom. Some spokesmen, like James H. Cone of Union Theological Seminary, contend that "the crisis in the black community is so critical that it would weaken the struggle to dilute it with a concern for whites; the black man's concern should be for self-liberation." Yet is complete separation at all possible, since there is a constant going and coming between the two communities? And is it possible to seek liberation in such a climate of separation, wherein you can conclude that

[3] *Ibid.*, p. 37.

"the white man no longer exists. He is not to be lived with and he is not to be destroyed. He is simply to be ignored"? [4]

Whatever methods may be adopted in the future civil rights struggle, a vast majority of black power advocates have long since lost faith in the nonviolent way. Calvin C. Hernton gave expression to this loss of faith when he wrote.

It is not nice or cultured for middle-class Negroes to fight, to be aggressive; they do not want to "embarrass" their oppressors, they do not want to appear "rude and uncultured" by confronting their oppressors head on. . . .

The species of the nonviolent Negro, as a progressive social force toward the liberation of black people in America, has been eclipsed by the very forces that have called the species into being and yet prevailed against it—the forces of compromise, corruption, hate and violence. Then, too, the socio-economic, political and cultural organism that is America, is a powerful octopus. It has proved itself capable of absorbing crisis after crisis throughout the world; and it has literally swallowed up the nonviolent movement, which now represents, at best, nothing more than obsolete idealism. [5]

Whites have been excluded from the black power movement because black people have come to feel that whites, no matter what their attitude, cannot do for the black man what he alone needs to do for himself. This conclusion was reached by SNCC workers in the summer of 1964, when hundreds of whites were at work in Mississippi. Many leaders were slow to realize that Negroes were responding only because the workers were white, and not because they were committed to the act. Julius Lester, a SNCC worker of that summer, put it this way:

[4] Stokely Carmichael, "What We Want," *New York Review of Books*, Autumn, 1966.

[5] In an essay "Dynamite out of Their Skulls," in *Black Fire*, ed. by LeRoi Jones and Larry Neal (New York: Morrow, 1968).

Whites, no matter how well meaning, could not relate to the Negro community. A Negro would follow a white person to the courthouse, not because he'd been convinced he should register to vote, but simply because he had been trained to say yes to whatever a white person wanted.[6]

From this point of view, it is not easy to differ with many of the conclusions that lead to separation, and it is clear why so many people feel that if liberation is to come, it must come from black people. It is much easier to understand some of the conclusions of black power when one looks for the logic. Much of the logic is derived from the bitter experiences that black men have had with the efforts of whites to help—efforts that did not contribute to the achievement of the selfhood that black awareness would suggest.

There is no current clear conception of God in much of the messianic hope as it is now in focus in the black community. The God concept is assumed as implied within the hope.

Black Awareness and the Color of God

There is current in the black community a widespread reaction against the tendency on the part of the white oppressor to project the image of a white God. This tendency has led many young black people to reject Christianity and to seek some other religious expression. Just what long-range effect this will have on the future of God within the context of the black church one cannot be sure. But too many blacks have contended that the black church has housed a God who could not be interested in the plight of the black man because he was white. They have contended that the black church

---

[6] "The Angry Children of Malcolm X," *Sing Out*, November, 1966.

adopted the God of the white church, and thus neither God nor the church have any relevancy for the black man's struggle for freedom and liberation. Some writers, like Joseph Washington, contend that the Negro's religion has been outside the mainstream of Christianity, more of a protest than a faith. At first many people were in great disagreement with Dr. Washington, but now they are recognizing current attempts to institutionalize black awareness, and one is seeing and hearing a somewhat more clearly articulated religious message. Older forms of ritual are being revised, and there are efforts to develop a theology more basic to the concept of black awareness. To date, very few churches have gone as far as Garvey's African Orthodox Church, but they are beginning to concern themselves about a religion that will be more acceptable to the ghettos. They are sure they need a God who will speak to the need for liberation, a God who will be more related to the black struggle. It will be a religion that is much more concerned with this world; it has very little need for heaven as such.

Probably no other group in America has approached the religious aspects of the ghetto as has Ron Karenga and his West Coast organization US. Karenga teaches that "we must concern ourselves more with plans for this life, rather than the next life which has its own problems, for the next life across Jordan is much further away, than the growl of dogs and the policemen and the pains of hunger and disease." [7]

While Karenga's religion is for this world, and its symbols are of the earth, it has very little to articulate concerning God. But in the work of Albert B. Cleage, Jr., a minister of the Central United Church of Christ, in Detroit, Michigan,

[7] Clide Halisi and James Mtume, eds., *The Quotable Karenga* (Los Angeles: US, 1967).

one sees coming to focus a kind of black Christology in the Church of the Black Madonna, wherein is articulated a new interpretation of Jesus. He is seen as a black man, he is a Zealot, and his messiahship is directed to the business of ministering to a black people. His mission is liberation—political, social, economic, and religious. Black-power Christianity is for now, and it is for real. As his book *The Black Messiah* makes plain, black religion is directed at political action, economic pressure, and black control of black communities. Jesus, as the Black Messiah, gives strength and revolutionary ardor to his followers.

The Black Messiah leaves much to be desired, if the book is intended to be a proof that Jesus was physically black, but it does cogently speak to the need for social and political action on the part of the black church. There is a strong emphasis on the "chosen people" idea, and the belief that God is fighting for the black man and with him as he fights. Cleage goes on to contend:

> When we march, when we take it to the streets in open conflict, we must understand that in the stamping feet and the thunder of violence we can hear the voice of God. When the Black Church accepts its role in the Black Revolution, it is able to understand and interpret revolutionary Christianity, and the revolution becomes a part of our Christian faith.[8]

In the writings of Cleage and other black awareness advocates, there is now not only a strong tendency to relate God to the black man's struggle; there is also the tendency to relate his color to the people oppressed. This began in Garvey's time, but it keeps coming back in new forms and with new emphases. Martin Luther King, Jr., and others with

[8] *The Black Messiah* (New York: Sheed & Ward, 1968), p. 6.

less noted theological background, related God to the struggle. But of late, God is being more and more identified with the struggle with reference to color. In much of the black community there is almost a complete rejection of any white art forms that would make God appear white. Black awareness is fast coming to the black church, and there is an effort to recolor God totally black. Cleage has done this with Jesus; others are doing it with God. This is because a white God, they contend, has tended to accept the meaning of blackness in its most degraded sense, and the Christian religion has not addressed itself ecclesiastically to the problems of being black in white America.

It is of interest to note here that there are many people in the black community itself who are concerned that advocates of black awareness will lead a struggling people in the direction of a new appropriation of the color of Jesus and maybe even of God. They are concerned that many of the art forms, symbols, and literature are reflecting more and more the color of the people of the black church. They consider this as anthropomorphic and thus unworthy of theological consideration. However, when one takes an objective view of the tendency, he is led to ask why not. The black man has a right to appropriate his God in his own color, and to express this in art forms, language symbols, and literature. Is this not a sign of maturity?

Indeed, when the oppressed no longer is satisfied to accept or adopt the God of the oppressor, especially his explicit or implicit color as it is expressed in art and literature, then the process of liberation has already begun. When an oppressed people are no longer willing to accept without question a religion or a God who accepts the idea of inequality for any part of the human family, is this not a sign of maturity?

Man has always appropriated his God in some sense of the

114

word. Ever since the dawn of human reason man has sought to know God. And through the ages men of religion or rational reflection have striven to comprehend the infinite nature of the Divine.

The black awareness search for God has been somewhat rationalistic in approach, and it seems to seek a refinement upon the notion of divinity. In the search to reinterpret the concept of God, or the object of that concept, in black art forms, the very character of God is being altered, so that the idea of God, for the black community, is becoming more and more identical with a personal and yet infinite and eternal Being. God, for the black awareness movement, is now no longer a totally transcendent deity, but a Divinity immanent in the black man's struggle. But then religion, for the black church, has never traditionally been merely theoretical and speculative; it has been practical as well. The God of the black man has had to distill and purify the dark experience of brutal oppression. Thus the search for God, for the black man, has never been a mere intellectual pastime; rather, it has been the result of an inner struggle, and it has been pursued with great and difficult effort. It is against the background of such a search that the black community is now coming to seek a God who is no longer the God of the white oppressor.

One wonders, however, what this altering of God's color will do for the black man. Will it make him, as a mature religious person, any more responsible with the use of his newly acquired black power than the white man was with his white power? Will the black man, with his black God, be a better man than the white man was with his white God? The deeper question may be, Will black man, as God's chosen, act any better than white man has acted? Indeed, is not the idea of God, no matter what his color, an indispensable prerequisite for man's ethical being? These questions are posed because they bring us to the final part of this book, which will suggest a higher theological stance for the current struggle. One realizes that in much of the black community the suggestion of such a position may be unacceptable to a large segment of black readers, especially those who are strong adherents of black power.

Those who advocate black awareness, and who would adhere to separatism as a means of achieving a true selfhood and the ultimate realization of authentic black self-identity, often ignore the fact that the humanity of man is much deeper than color. It is true that there is great need for the strengths that can be derived from all that is good in the civil rights struggle. It is true that there is need for the self-esteem that black awareness teaches. But the ultimate manhood or personhood sought should be, under God, fully human. The deeper question is whether it is possible for God to acquire color without becoming identified with that which is too narrow to be fully representative of the total human family, much less that which is Divine. All that we know in man is relative, but that which we conceive in God is normative. This is the inherent danger in representing God in any human conception, either concrete or abstract.

The much greater danger in all the current tendency on the part of advocates of black awareness to recolor God is that in the process of recoloring, those who do so may well alter the very concept of being itself. And in so doing, the God of black awareness may become a mere idol god of a folk religion, a god who is only interested in the welfare of a black people, a god who will deliver a special people from a special oppressor. It must be remembered that folk religion, even without a clearly identified god concept, can foster

116

brotherhood, social solidarity, and many other things that are now being promoted within the black community.

Many adherents of the Christian tradition, especially those who have long since been mature enough not to relate God to any particular color, see the danger of the religion of black awareness becoming a cultural manifestation, with God as true living Reality colored out and replaced by a more narrowly conceived God of group interest. The religion of the black community would then be a cult of black awareness, void of true redemptive mission.

If the traditional Christian gospel of the black church is to survive within the black community, then it must assume its rightful responsibility in the liberation of the black man. If this unique role is to be assumed, the gospel of the black church must address itself to the following problems, which are live options at every level of community structure.

First of all, the gospel must address itself to the problems of changing the connotation of blackness in relation to a black people. Blackness, as a concept, has too long been related to all that is unclean, degraded, and undesirable.

Second, the concept of blackness has also acquired some theological meanings, which, when applied to persons, are degrading morally and spiritually. The Bible has been used in the process of dehumanizing people, because it has served as a proof text for inequality. Evil and sin have become so much associated with blackness that it is no wonder black people are associated with uncleanliness or wickedness almost unconsciously within the minds of many white Christians. This means that the gospel must address itself to the radical task of building a new structure of language symbols for the concept of blackness so as to offset the almost unconscious tendency to apply it, in its degrading sense, to human beings.

Third, the gospel of black awareness must find a new lan-

117

guage of hope for the ghetto, a new language of the people, understood by the people, to the end that it will indeed be the good news of liberation and of radical change. It must be a language that will generate a kind of race pride that will make a difference in all aspects of life, conduct, and attitude. Much of the language of the black awareness movement is of the people; this is why it has the potential of such a great appeal.

Finally, no gospel of black awareness should ignore the basic tenets of the Judeo-Christian faith. To do so would be merely to establish a folk religion that would not survive the test of history. The gospel must seek always to clarify the issues that are in focus in the struggle, while at the same time adhering to the faith tradition. If a new theological language of black awareness is not found which will give meaning and validity to the movement beyond that which is now implied, then the present trends will continue, and the black man will have lost the God who brought him over so many difficult places in the past.

Black Liberation and a God Who Takes Sides

It has been suggested above that a God who is merely black or merely white cannot be an adequate God-concept upon which all peoples of the world can stake their ultimate hope. He is simply too small to be conceived as the Father of the human race. This is not to say that a group is not free to relate their interest and their concerns to their own particular needs. Relevant appropriation is one thing, but reductionism and narrow identification can only lead to anthropomorphic concepts of God which are too narrow for an adequate faith commitment.

However, closely related to the tendency in the black community to color God black is also the tendency to commit God to the side of the black man and to make of him a God who is only concerned for the liberation of black people. Such a concept of God has been derived partly from the Old Testament conception of God, and partly from a radical reinterpretation of the person and work of Jesus.

Probably, more than the two tendencies cited above, the tendency to identify God with a particular cause or a particular people has always had great psychological appeal for those who were a part of the particular cause or the particular people. There would be a great weakness in the current literature of black theology if it did not inform black people of the meaning of God's will for all people. To be sure, theology must be concerned with securing for the black man's aspirations the blessings of God, but these blessings cannot be only for God's chosen people; they must be for the whole human family. Indeed, how easy it would be for the black man to acquire, because of the special attention given him by study, politicians, the church, civic organizations, etc. (not equal treatment, but special treatment), a kind of belief that he is especially worthy of God's benevolence and even of God's intervention in revolutionary struggles. To cite such a danger is not to suggest that God should be conceived as a mere heavenly guarantor of the status quo. But neither is it to say that he is the avenging God of the offended, and such a view is what one may well be hearing in too much of current theology in general and black theology in particular. Indeed, how many people forget that "God maketh his sun to rise on the evil and on the good."

When one reads much of black theology now, there is a concern that God is being placed on the side of black people only, without compromise or willingness to recognize him as being the God of the enemy as well. James Cone, makes this point clear when he asserts that

this is the key to Black Theology. It refuses to embrace any concept of God which makes black suffering the will of God. Black people should not accept slavery, lynching, or any form of injustice as tending to good. It is not permissible to appeal to the idea that God's will is inscrutable or that the righteous sufferer will be rewarded in heaven. If God has made the world in which black people *must* suffer, and if he is a God who rules, guides, and sanctifies the world, then he is a murderer. To be the God of black people, he must be against the oppression of black people.[9]

Dr. Cone by over-identification tends to give the impression that God is only on the black man's side. Again, it might also be seen in his tendency to extend authenticity only to the church that engages in the liberation of the black man.[10] In a moving statement, he contends that

it is the job of the Church to become black with him and accept the shame which white society places on blacks. But the Church knows that what is shame to the world is holiness to God. Black is holy, that is, it is a symbol of God's presence in history on behalf of the oppressed man. Where there is black, there is oppression; but blacks can be assured that where there is blackness, there is Christ who has taken on blackness so that what is evil in man's eyes might become good. Therefore Christ is black because he is oppressed, and oppressed because he is black. And if the Church is to join Christ by following his opening, it too must go where suffering is and become black also.[11]

Other examples of the tendency to identify God with the

---

[9] Cone, *Black Theology and Black Power*, p. 124.
[10] *Ibid.*, Chapter III.
[11] *Ibid.*, p. 69.

side of the black man are given in Albert B. Cleage's *Black Messiah*, cited earlier, in which he contends that Jesus was a black man with a mission of liberation and freedom for a New Testament people who were themselves black.

Larger expressions of the attempt to make God a part of revolution and to place him on the side of the oppressed are to be found in S. G. F. Brandon's book, *Jesus and the Zealots*,[12] in which he contends that Jesus was a Zealot and only concerned with the political situation of his times. Somewhat on the strength of Brandon's book and the Jewish historian Josephus' books, *The Works of Josephus* and *The Antiquities of the Jews*, Colin Morris' book, *Unyoung, Uncolored, Unpoor*, is a classic example of placing God on the side of the revolutionary. His radical interpretation of Jesus and his clear identification of God with revolution is clearly seen in his book's radical support of revolution. The extreme expression of such a view is seen in his contention that "hence, *Salvation by Violence!* may not be so far wide of the mark. God is the inspiration of every strategy which breaks down the old to make way for the new. He is behind *all* the revolutions of our time. Not every one of them is achieved by violence, but many are." [13]

As one reads black theology and other, broader literature of black awareness, the question that comes back time and time again is whether the black man, in moving toward an ideology of revolution as the only means by which he can become free, is really serious about God's involvement in revolution and how God is related to the struggle. If, as has already been pointed out, black theology attempts a theology of revolution, if those who contend for such an emphasis

---

[12] (Manchester: Manchester University Press, 1967.)
[13] Morris, *Unyoung, Uncolored, Unpoor*, p. 142.

121

try to relate the "new thing" God is doing to what he has done before, then the question is, How will it differ from the Western man's thirst for explanations that are prone to locate God in the ultimate "why" of things and events instead of in the more immediate "how" of things and events? Colin Morris may well be right, when he asserts that

the Christian who becomes a revolutionary takes the risk that in a world locked up in the past, the blow which opens the way to the future may count as the "one thing needful" about which Jesus talked. He steps beyond any traditional understanding of Jesus into a spiritual and ethical No Man's Land in the hope that the future is where God is.[14]

Such is noble talk, but as one looks at what is taking place among those who live with the revolutionary zeal, he wonders if indeed their religion can sustain them against the ever-present danger of becoming true revolutionaries in the sense of the description given in 1868 by an anonymous author of a short pamphlet called *The Revolutionary Catechism*:

The revolutionary is a dedicated man. He has no interests, no business, no emotions, no attachments, no property, not even a name. In his innermost depths he has broken all ties with the social order. He knows but one science, that of destruction. The tender sentiments of family, friendship, love and gratitude must be subjugated to the single cold passion of the revolutionary cause.[15]

There is still a greater danger for those who would seek to reduce the concept of God to the manageable level of a

[14] *Ibid.*, p. 157.
[15] Quoted by Roland Gaucher, *The Terrorists, from Tsarist Russia to the O.A.S.* (London: Secker & Warburg, 1968), p. 3.

complete identification with the revolutionary cause and with a revolutionary people. Morris is on much clearer theological, and indeed nearer traditional Christian, ground when he asserts:

Without warping his character, man cannot make a single good —not even social justice—the central business of living, with everything else relegated to a subordinate place. Unreasonableness is the essential attitude of extremism, for those who see reason cease to be extreme and are lost to the cause.[16]

After reading such a book and fixing on such sections, one wonders if reason alone is sufficient in these days: If God is identified with the true spirit of revolution, and actions call one far out beyond the frontiers of faith, where is the safe ground upon which to build a future for people who dare wish for a future in this world and in this lifetime? Are the seeds of hope in mere revolution?

Black Liberation and the Concept of God for a World Come of Age

The black community has long since abandoned the idea of suffering any more at the hands of the oppressor. However, in the search for a usable concept of God, some consideration must be given to his relationship to suffering and the sufferer. Is God to be separated from the black man's struggle, is he to be made a part of it by taking sides, or is he to be thought of as a being totally unrelated to the black man's condition in the world?

From his prison walls Bonhoeffer offered the idea of shared suffering with a God who seems to be in process of weaning

---

[16] Morris, *Unyoung, Uncolored, Unpoor*, p. 156.

the world of its over-dependence upon him. On July 16, 1944, he wrote to Eberhard Bethge:

The God who lets us live in the world without the working hypothesis of God is the God before whom we stand continually. Before God and with God we live without God. God lets himself be pushed out of the world on to the cross. He is weak and powerless in the world, and this is precisely the way, the only way, in which he is with us and helps us. Matthew 8:17 makes it quite clear that Christ helps us, not by virtue of his own omnipotence, but by the virtue of his weakness and suffering.[17]

Here there is a call for a mature God concept, for to contend that God himself is helpless to relieve those who suffer at the hands of a ruthless enemy is to ask for a different kind of faith than that which is traditionally characterized in the black church. What does it mean to remind a black man, with Bonhoeffer, that "we are not Christ, but if we want to be Christian, we must have some share in Christ's large-heartedness by acting with responsibility and in freedom when the hour of danger comes. . . . The Christian is called to sympathy and action, not in the first place by his own suffering, but by the suffering of his brethren, for whose sake Christ suffered." [18]

This may not say what many black Christians would like said, and probably, because it came from the lips of an alien theologian, many blacks will find it hard to accept. But the message is great, and it puts the sufferer in business for "others," and that makes all the difference in the world. Indeed, Bonhoeffer has greatly helped us create a contemporary definition of God—not as a haughty, omnipotent

[17] Dietrich Bonhoeffer, *Letters and Papers from Prison*, ed. by Eberhard Bethge (New York: Macmillan, 1967), pp. 1-17.
  [18] *Ibid.*

deity of the Middle Ages, but a God sharing fully in his creation and thus, too, in the real sufferings of his world.

Bonhoeffer futher contends that Christians stand by God in his hour of grieving; that is what distinguishes Christians from pagans. Jesus asked in Gethsemane, "Could ye not watch with me one hour?" That is a reversal of what religious man expects from Cod. Man is summoned to share in God's sufferings at the hands of a godless world. He must therefore really live as a mature person in a godless world, without attempting to gloss over or explain its ungodliness in some religious way or other. He must live a "secular" life, and thereby share in God's sufferings. To be a Christian means, not to be religious in a particular way, but to be the man that Christ creates in us.[19] It is not the religious act that makes the Christian, but participation in the sufferings of God in the secular life.

What does such a concept of God mean for the black man's struggle? To such a question, the simple answer may lie in the fact that man does not expect that God will come down from above and undo all wrongs for him. Neither does it mean that he must with God face all that is not right with the world and with him participate in helping to right all the wrongs. Surely, it would mean that one should not become bitter and resentful to the point of calling for exceptions in his case. But to be a man, in a Christian sense, means to stand up and go after that which by God belongs to you. It may well mean a much more religious stance in the world of the white man, but it will be one very much different from the traditional religious stance of the black man. The black man, in taking this stance, will not presuppose that God is on his

19 *Ibid.*

side, but rather will presuppose that he is on God's side. Such a stance will mean a different kind of maturity. Standing in such security, assured that he is with God, the black man will find that to pray "Father forgive them!" is a natural expression.

When one talks of such a security, the kind that Bonhoeffer's letters would suggest, then one is talking about a different kind of man in the world. It is a manhood that cannot be subjugated, and one that cannot be rejected, for it is radically different from those who have not reached such a religious maturity. One can see in the religion of black power too much of a fixing on the black man, too much of a concern for him in his own struggle, and probably too much of a calling for help. It seems that a more mature conception of God would reveal a more mature man who is harder to subject to any status less than equal.

One must contend that much that has happened to the black man was because of the white man, but much more that has happened to him was because he allowed it to take place. Within the movement of black awareness there is the hope that there is now budding a new kind of manhood—a new kind of manhood that will demand a different kind of recognition and respect. It is upon this foundation that any hope for the black community must be built.

Toward a More Adequate Concept of God for the Black Awareness Revolution

In concluding this section, one must point out that a new concept of God is made important only as a new type of black man takes shape. It is not altogether true that the type of black man conceived determines the kind of concept of God that is needed for the black community. However, in reading the current mood of the black community, one must conclude that the two are related to a point where they cannot be totally separated.

In a very real sense, an adequate hope for the black community must rest upon a God concept that will embrace or catch up in its meaning all the aspirations of the black man for the now and for the not-yet of the future. When a black man or any man seeks a God without hope or a future without God, not only is the foundation of his hope in danger, but the very structure of human existence is being assailed. In an age of collectivism, when the tendency is to translate individual hope into the social process, there is a danger that many who adhere to violence will see the ultimate goals of black aspiration as being worthy of the sacrifice of individual life and concerns. Religion as hope is the human quest for fulfillment beyond the present experiences of alienation and destruction within each individual, and within the collective life. Black religion as hope is also related to the possibility of black man's becoming truly fulfilled beyond the deformities of his past. Such a past, rooted in the black experience, and a present, pregnant with hope, calls him to the future, especially beyond the inevitability of his current despair. Indeed, do not man's hopes, if they are rooted in an adequate concept of God for his time, always burst open his present, driving him beyond existing frontiers to search the horizons for an ever-new reality? If man does not hope or need to hope, then what sense does it make for anyone to speak of God? If the God conceived is not adequate, if there are no needs in man and his world which still cry out to be filled, or if all needs can adequately be filled by man himself, then either God has become obsolete or the day of total human fulfillment has already arrived. If there is no hope in the black community, then the question of God will not even arise. Any God who is invoked as the answer to human needs, no matter what they are, is irrelevant in a world that has grown beyond the point of a sense of needing him.

The goals of the black awareness movement will fall far short of fulfillment if the movement is not rooted in a God of the future. He must be a God who is strong enough to determine the outcome of the future both within and beyond history. There is no future in a God who, at any point, gives up his creation. For God to be adequate for the now and the not-yet of the black man's future, he must transcend the now and the not-yet in history. He must be a God who is active on man's behalf; he must be a God who is himself engaged in the cosmic battle with evil. If he is thought to be so related to man, then the problem of evil is put on a totally different plane. In the black community, God's righteousness is his power in relation to men who are not in the right, who do not do what is right, who violate the rights of others in self-righteous aggression, who rob God of his rights, his due, by putting him down in their pride. This is not the way many black men see the white man's God.

The image of God's reality and of his future becomes present only where righteousness reigns on earth. The core of his righteousness is justice infused with love. Where God's love is not able to do its work freely, it employs other means such as protest, instruments of law, threats, and punishment. At many points in history, God puts on the ugly mass of his wrath to pressure people to satisfy the needs of others, even when they do not feel like it. Indeed, it is all too true that men, white or black, often do not freely live for others; they too often live for themselves. The future of God, if properly conceived, rejects as its adversary everything and everybody that refuses to seek the fullness of life for self and others.

In this sense, every person is committed with God to the fulfillment of others. Such a commitment means not only that one will contribute to the growth of others, but that he is obligated to allow others the freedom for such development without obstructions. To do otherwise is to invite God's wrath. But the God whose wrath is provoked is also the God of even those who have, by their very acts of evil, invited God's disfavor. God then is the redeemer of the oppressed as well as of the oppressor; he joins the struggle on both sides, seeking to transform both the oppressed and the oppressor.

God, for the black community, must be at work in a visible sort of way. Especially, he must be seen in the progressive development toward a better social lot for a people oppressed. Therefore, any adequate God concept cannot be conceived in the narrow and restricted sense of any particular that does not also relate to all. He cannot be for the black man only, just as he cannot be for the white man only. He must be a God for all, and his concerns must be equally related to all. It is every black man's Christian calling to fight against all the ills and woes that afflict mankind and against their human causes and provocations. To leave misery unalleviated, to leave social revolution to the angry and the selfish, to stand aloof from the agonies of the new world aborning is to make it all too plain that one is not interested in the compassion of God, but only in our own passive hope of his impossible providence. For the black community, there can be but one answer, joined by all the past heroes of the faith, to the problems of evil. It is disconcertingly simple: Evil is overcome by the intelligent, competent concern and actions of people who are willing to pay the price of the conflict. To be sure, there is no "Utopia of the beyond" which does not have a real life relation to the present conditions of history. In a real sense then, no future of history can be merely quantitatively new, it must also be qualitatively new. Faith in God does not supplant history so that present conditions become an insignificant matter to believers; neither should involvement in history so absorb the black man of faith that he forgets God's place in the current struggle. Because he can hope in the future, he can best, under God, oppose the dehumanizing schemes of this world and the systems of the present to the point of perfecting meaningful change.

The danger of the black man's current religious mood is that it may attempt to exclude God from the struggle, and by so doing exclude the power of the future. The temptations of the black man's current attitude consist not so much in the titantic desire to be like God, but in his weakness, timidity, and weariness, not wanting to do what God requires of him.

God has exalted man and given him the prospect of a life that is wide and free, but man too often hangs back and lets himself down. God, as the power of the future, promises a new creation of all things in righteousness and peace. But too many men act as if everything was as before, and they remain as before. God honors black man with his promises, but black man too often does not believe himself capable of what God has required of him. This lack of self-confidence is the one sin that most profoundly threatens the black believer. It is not the evil he does, but the good he does not do, not his misdeeds but his omissions of great deeds, that accuse him most congently. They accuse him of lack of hope. For the sin of the omission of great deeds has its ground in hopelessness and weakness of faith. To hope is to become a new person fit for great deeds. There dawns within the being of black man the making of a new counter-personhood capable of the needed black and white confrontation. This encounter, and the outcome of it, may well determine the future of the country and the future of black-white relations in the world.

9

COMMUNITY BEYOND RACISM

Any Christian hope, current in such a world of despair, must be a hope that has been internalized to the point where it makes of the adherent a new being in the fullest ontological sense. By and large, such a hope must be positive if it is to prove adequate as a foundation for authentic selfhood. While black awareness, as a movement, has not reached its fullest potential, it still is a sufficient concept upon which to build the hope of a people. But too much of the black experience of the past has been articulated in a totally negative literature, while it should have taken on a positive potential. To become a concept of hope, it would seem, the concept of black selfhood must become a forward concept, divesting itself of much of the personal doubts and uncertainties of the past. It must get beyond the bitterness of the past; it must fix on the intentions and possibilities of the future. Black theology, to become a theology of hope, must fix on the forward intentions of the black man. Indeed, is it not true that "whoever does not meet a man at this level of his being knows nothing deeply significant about him. Having met him 'there' everything else about him is stamped with the unique quality of his own transcendence. He is seen no longer as a simple prolongment of his background, but rather is known in his possible surpassingness." [1]

Christian hope is futuristic, then, in the sense that it fixes on the forwardness of selfhood. Heraclitus was right when he reminded us that "he who does not hope for the unexpected, will not find it." Hope alone is called realistic for the simple reason that it alone takes seriously the possibilities with which all reality is fraught. It takes things not as they happen to be, but rather as progressive, moving things with possibilities of change. Only as long as racism exists and peoples of different skins are in a fragmented and, at times, experimental state that is not yet resolved, is there any sense in earthly hope? Black awareness, in its truest sense, anticipates what is possible to reality; historic and moving as it is, those who adhere to the concept are under mandate to use their influence to help decide the processes of the future. Thus the hopes and the anticipations of the future are not a transfiguring glow superimposed upon a darkened existence, as some current black theologians would have us believe, but are realistic ways of perceiving the scope of our possibilities; and as such they set everything in motion and keep it in a state of change. Black people can achieve change. They have a right to hope only if in their eyes the world is full of all kinds of possibilities, namely all the possibilities ordained by the God of hope. Black people have a right to hope only if they see reality and mankind, white and black, in the hands of him whose voice calls into history from its end, saying, "Behold, I make all things new," and only if, from hearing this word of promise, they acquire the freedom to renew life here and change the face of the earth.

[1] Ray L. Hart, *Unfinished Man and the Imagination* (New York: Herder and Herder, 1968), pp. 143-44.

It is true, as Moltmann has suggested, that "the most serious objection to a theology of hope springs not from presumption or despair, for these two basic attitudes of human existence presuppose hope, but the objection to hope arises from the religion of humble acquiescence in the present." [2]

Too much of the literature of the religion of black power, black awareness, and even black theology is void of hope; it is so bogged down in attempting to articulate what is wrong with the lot of the black peoples of the pro-white world that it may forget to ask the question:

Is it not always in the present alone that man is truly existent, real, contemporary with himself, acquiescent and certain? Memory binds him to the past that no longer is. Hope casts him upon the future that is not yet. He remembers having lived, but he does not live. He remembers having loved, but he does not love. He remembers the thoughts of others, but he does not think. It seems to be the same with him in hope. He hopes to live, but he does not live. He expects to be happy one day, and this expectation causes him to pass over the happiness of the present. He is never, in memory and hope, wholly himself and wholly in his present. Always he either limps behind it or hastens ahead of it. Memories and hopes appear to cheat him of the happiness of being undividedly present. They rob him of his present and drag him into times that no longer exist or do not yet exist. They surrender him to the non-existent and abandon him to vanity. For these times subject him to the stream of transience—the stream that sweeps him to annihilation. [3]

Faith in God brings a new dimension to life, a result of the fact that one has tuned in to the nearness of God, for living amid the simple everyday things of today is, of course, living

---

[2] Moltmann, *Theology of Hope*, p. 26.
[3] *Ibid.*

in the fullness of time and in the nearness of God. However, to know the fullness of God is to grasp the never-returning moment, to be wholly at one with oneself, wholly self-possessed and on the mark. He is, as Paul says, the God who raises the dead and calls into being the things that are not (Rom. 4-17). This God is present where we wait in hope upon his promises and transformation. When we have faith in a God who calls into being things that are not, then the things that are not yet, that are the future, become "thinkable" because they can be hoped for.

Under God, there is possible such a positive, forward thrust in black awareness for many reasons. This is what is meant by "being-toward." Man in general, and especially black man now, has his being vouchsafed to him not as a possession but only as a being-toward, which is a positive commitment to what Carl E. Braaten calls "the power of the future." [4]

Christian hope, as it is inherent in black awareness, gives the movement a teleological dimension because of its tendency of being-toward and because of the prospects that such a tendency creates for further actions. Such a tendency, if it is a part of the mind-set of the black mood of thinking, enables the adherent to anticipate the possibilities that the future holds, avoiding either false optimism or premature despair.

Having spoken of the possibilities of black awareness, as a concept that commits its adherents to a teleological future, we must admit that there are certain characteristics that have to be related and explained, if they are to be understood as facets of a theology of hope.

1. First of all, black awareness is humanistic in the Ernst Bloch sense of a theology of hope, and yet it is more than

[4] See his *Future of God* (New York: Harper, 1969), pp. 59 ff.

135

mere humanism or naturalism in relation to the black man's hope under God. While no black theologian knowledgeable of the current aspirations of the black community would ignore the "this-world" concerns of black people's hopes, he could not agree with Bloch when he contends that religion can well be conceived of as mere "meta-religion," inherited and void of a "God-reference" which transcends mere hope or human aspirations.[5] Even in the "religion of black power," as Vincent Harding characterizes it in *The Religious Situation 1968*, there is a strong God-Entity implicit, even if not admitted by many exponents of the ideology.

Having concluded that black awareness starts with the individual and his inner conception of himself under God, such a conclusion makes sense only as it relates to a God-Entity for the simple reason that so much of the cultural ethos that has declared the black man inferior and treated him as such was derived from erroneous religious beliefs. Black awareness appeals to the inner core of being with a stress on authentic black self-identity. It is what H. Richard Niebuhr calls "an active thing, a committing of self to something, an anticipation. It is directed toward something that is active, that has power or is power." [6] If it is true that by one's active response he affirms God's intention, then black awareness commits its adherents to the power of God, whether affirmed or not. Through it alone can black people, who were once thought unworthy, join the human family by the force of being-forward. Is this not freedom under God in its primary meaning? The exercise of such power will create the conditions for meaningful relationships. It is being-forward with

---

[5] See Moltmann's *Religion, Revolution and the Future*, pp. 148 ff.

[6] H. Richard Niebuhr, *Radical Monotheism and Western Culture* (New York: Harper, 1943), p. 117.

such ontological weight that one preserves his personal integrity within the human context. This involves at least the limited power sufficient to act out one's own intentions.

2. Second, under the mandate of hope, black awareness literature has a strong sense of messianic mission. Whether it is theological or nontheological in nature, there is a sense in which black men think they are called of God to deliver black America from its bondage and white America from its lethal folly. The Marcus Garvey movement seemingly has taken on new life in our time, and it may well be that Ronald Fair is not too far wrong when he contends that "every black man in this country is aware that our time has come." Indeed there is a new wind of freedom astir within the black community so that this current period in history is the fullness of time in many black minds. This aspect of hope has been mentioned earlier, but in this final chapter an additional word is needed to say what this means when such a belief is conceived under God.

From Garvey to Cleage there have been those who have related their hope to more elementary concerns, such as the color and the locus of God. Now there comes the much more mature concern about what blackness under God means. Whether we recognize it or not, it would seem that the black man's time has come in America, and many who now linger in bitterness have not been aware of what is taking place. There are many black people who voice no hope. One need only recall that blackness as a concept is being included rather than excluded at more points now than at any other time in history. It is interesting that this should be so at a time when many black people are talking separatism. Television and the business world are at one in the current movement to include blackness. Job opportunities are being extended in broader scope, though now there is a cry by many for a rejection of the establishment in favor of goals within the narrow confines of the black community. The tide of history seems to be toward some kind of inclusion of the black man in spite of all that either racial group can do or say. The only question that remains is, How shall inclusiveness be achieved? The word "achieved" is used to prevent the impression that these signs of progress are without struggle and confrontation between black and white people who have not come to a mutual agreement in their respective commitment to change.

The time has come when the black man and the white man must decide to sit down together and come to grips with the problem of racism, else the racism that now rages so deep in American life will surely end in violence, and no one will be the better. History has set the two, black and white, on a confrontation course, and the point of contact will be either one of violent conflict or one of dialogue and mutual agreement. The black awareness movement has so matured the black community that it will not accept a compromise for less than a better lot for all.

A strange thing is happening to blackness as it is being included at almost every level of the commercial world. The concept of blackness is being accepted and commercialized, but one is not too certain at this point whether this is being done without accepting black people. There are many signs that the white business world has fixed on blackness as a concept, that there is willingness to include it on television and in advertisements simply because there is money to be made by appealing to the black community. In spite of progress at the level of inclusion, little progress is visible at the level of a full acceptance of black personhood.

3. Third, black awareness is characterized by the lack of a centralized programmatic thrust. At the moment there are many who would offer some type of program under the gen-

eral label of protest, but there is no one overall civil rights program that now unites all black people and commits them to one way of achieving the white man's acceptance of the black man's full personhood. Even a black theology of hope can but ask, Is this part of the process of coming of age? Is this a part of a coming of age when the black man's struggle must reveal itself in many, many facets, each a part of one total overall thrust of human blackness struggling to be recognized within the context of the family of God? For the black awareness movement, rightly interpreted—the emergence of black selfhood—is not to be taken or conceived as a thing in itself; rather it is to be viewed against the background of an emergent community. The Judeo-Christian faith, considering that man, black or white, finds himself in history and on a pilgrimage toward selfhood and community, gives some hints about how men ought learn to live together while they are realizing that promise. It is never a mandate to self alone; it is always an openness toward others. Selfhood is not self-evidence; in other words, one can be himself only when he has the benefit of a community of judgment. The Christian ethic, when it confers selfhood upon a man, should insist that a realistic self-judgment, the marrow of divine judgment, be part of that selfhood.

Whether there be one programmatic thrust makes little difference to many; the important thing is that the ultimate concern is for community wherein all can share as equals. Running through all the expressions of the black awareness movement there is the underlying concession that this is a common hope beyond protest or the need for struggle. The spirit in the air at the moment is one of impatience, frustration, and a desire to get on with things, to sweep aside the dead customs of the past and the arrangements that preserve injustice. At least, that is the spirit among the disinherited, those who have not yet been able to participate meaningfully in the equality revolution. It may well be that it is their impatience, rather than the conservatism of those restless people who resist, that is going to achieve the true community for which black people yearn.

Every black child has a right to ask, Why can't we change it all, and do so now? This is the mood among the movers and shakers. And they are not all black. Up to now, much of the resistance and blockage of progress has merely been reluctantly tolerated—by the black man, by the students, by the people of the Third World. That this patience was nearing an end has been shown not only by the nonviolent movement of the recent past, but also, in more dramatic ways, by the eruption of the black power movement, and the campus insurrections of more contemporary days. Now the time has come when changes have to be pushed through into reality whether all parties in the community are ready for them or not. Hope is seen in the fact that such a time has come, no matter what the opposition.

In the last section on "hopes," in his book *Public Ethics*, James Sellers gives two theological points concerning short-term prospects for the current black theology of hope which should be seen in the light of the tendency toward despair. The first is that history does bring the really new, but never the Kingdom of God in its fullness. "Part of the realization of the promise is in the struggle. Put this way, this is not a sentiment that revolutionaries have usually wanted to reckon with," [7] and who could blame them. Indeed, history, Sellers further contends, will never change men so much that they

[7] James Sellers, *Public Ethics: American Morals and Manners* (New York: Harper, 1970), p. 309.

are not finite any more, so much that they are not tempted to want more, so much that they can really get interested in the destinies of other men besides themselves. Is that too harsh, one would ask? Sellers thinks not; he cites four great political revolutions of the modern world—the American, the English, the French, and the Russian. He contends that none of them brought enough change, none of them failed to bring some change, but none brought the whole vision to reality. Certainly none of them, according to Sellers, left its beneficiaries able to love one another. Perhaps it did improve the prospects of justice in each case. And each kept alive hope in the future. If the American Revolution had brought all that is really promised in the Declaration of Independence, for example, surely the black man's struggle would not be considered the nation's number one unsolved domestic problem today.[8] The second point is that in any revolution the full-blown ideals themselves take time to emerge. As Preston Valien puts it in his essay, "The Montgomery Bus Protest as a Social Movement," while such a movement begins with a concrete incident, "it develops an ideology which progressively becomes more idealistic with the passage of time. And so as late as April, 1956, Martin Luther King, Jr., was suggesting that the black man in Montgomery sought the right, under segregation, to seat ourselves from the rear forward on a first-come, first-served basis." [9] But by 1963 the goals had taken on far more profound dimensions, as this later statement of King illustrates: "We're through with tokenism and gradualism and see-how-far-you've comeism. We're through

[8] *Ibid.*
[9] In *Race Relations: Problems and Theory,* ed. Jitsuichi Masuoka and Preston Valien (Chapel Hill: University of North Carolina Press, 1961), p. 116.

141

with we've-done-more-for-your-people-than-anyone-elseism. We can't wait any longer. Now is the time." [10]

In his book *The Fire Next Time*, James Baldwin articulates in clear theological language the ideal that is a part of the ethos of hope to which so many black people cling, even when there is nothing but despair. The small handful who are concerned may yet be able at this late hour, he says, "to end the racial nightmare, and achieve our country, and change the history of the world." [11]

Here is the test to which Christianity and the Christian ethics are put in our time. "If the concept of God has any validity or any use," says Baldwin, "it can only be to make us larger, freer, and more loving. If God cannot do this, then it is time we get rid of Him." [12] That is also to be said of religion itself—this force that seems to be not too far from the heart of every revolution—even the religion of black power, which is especially close to the black revolution. However, sadly, religion is also to be seen at the center of every resistance to the emergence of man, more certain if that which is emerging is new.

4. Finally, no black theologian can miss the fact that we move, as if we were indeed under some power of the future, toward some larger context wherein every person, race, or ethnic group shall take comfort in the fact of separateness and difference. Identity will be no problem, for identity will have been achieved within a climate wherein it will be fully recognized, fully accepted, and fully respected. There will be a pluralism of ideologies, interests, aims and aspirations, and

[10] *Time*, June 21, 1963, p. 14.
[11] Baldwin, *The Fire Next Time* (New York: Dial Press, 1963), p. 119.
[12] *Ibid*.

personhood; and no one will for any purpose be denied opportunity to achieve, or be excluded from community.

Such a climate, however, will not exclude the emergence of new concerns, new struggles, new aspirations, and a yearning for even newer levels of maturity. Let this tomorrow, this future day, be nearer the ideal of the Creator of the hope that compels such a dream.